Diderot and a Poetics of Science

Reading Plus

Mary Ann Caws
General Editor

Vol. 1

PETER LANG
New York · Berne · Frankfurt am Main

Suzanne L. Pucci

Diderot and a
Poetics of Science

PETER LANG
New York · Berne · Frankfurt am Main

848
D55xp

Library of Congress Cataloging-in-Publication Data

Pucci, Suzanne L.
  Diderot and a Poetics of Science.

  (Reading Plus ; vol. 1)
  Bibliography: p.
  Includes Index
    1. Diderot, Denis, 1713–1784—Style. 2. Poetics. 3. Science—
France—History—18th century. 4. Science—Philosophy.
I. Title II. Series.
PQ1979.P83   1986   848'.509   86-15394
ISBN 0-8204-0293-1
ISSN 0882-6196

CIP-Kurztitelaufnahme der Deutschen Bibliothek
Pucci, Suzanne L.:
Diderot and a Poetics of Science / Suzanne L. Pucci. –
New York ; Berne ; Frankfurt am Main : Lang, 1986.
  (Reading Plus ; Vol. 1)
  ISBN 0-8204-0293-1

NE: GT

88- 1497

Grateful acknowledgement is due to **Symposium**, 35 (4), 225–240
(1981–1982), a publication of the Helen Dwight Reid Educational
Foundation, for permission to employ portions of the author's article "Metamorphosis and Metaphor in Diderot's
Rêve de D'Alembert".

Printed by Weihert-Druck GmbH, Darmstadt (West Germany)

For Emilia and Giovanni

Contents

Preface

To conduct an inquiry into Denis Diderot's theory and methodology of science, I might have chosen several other texts as well as his *De l'Interprétation de la nature*, which constitutes the central focus of this book. But my study does not claim to offer a comprehensive view of the *philosophe*'s scientific endeavors. Nor is its ostensible goal to situate Diderot's writing within the schemas outlined by the history of science. Yet, it is not by chance that my project concentrates on a treatise cited perhaps more than any other in the annals of intellectual history for its role in registering and in accomplishing a shift to the method of experimental science and philosophy in eighteenth-century France. For in advocating that scientific and philosophical concepts be relegated to the testing ground of experimentation in the domain of nature's material reality, *De l'Interprétation de la nature* simultaneously and of necessity poses the epistemological as well as literary problematic of representation whose textual resolutions and strategies constitute a poetics of science.

"La philosophie expérimentale," following Diderot's terminology and thesis, serves as a corrective to the prescriptions and predictions of rationalist systems by involving not only the experimentation but the perceptual as well as cognitive experience of each interpreter of nature. To the extent that Diderot's method revolves around the relation between philosophical concept and perception, it also posits both explicitly and implicitly the relation between language and its objects, between the subject and object of experiment—problems that are identifiable as constitutive of a theory of knowledge or epistemology.

The methodology advanced in *De l'Interprétation de la nature* is concerned at a thematic and at a textual level as much with a description and definition of the properties of an experimenting, observing subject as with the all-important and newly (re)discovered objects of investigation in nature. Following Descartes' foundation of all thought and knowledge in the *cogito* of the *Méditations*, the *philosophes* of the eighteenth century attempted to establish the parameters of this principle of the subject by confronting it with the domain of a material, independent reality which, as Diderot's text demonstrates, this same principle of individual consciousness was essential in articulating (chs. 2 and 3).

Locke and Condillac as well as Diderot were concerned with what lies outside man's merely conceptual framework and consequently beyond his related linguistic conventions. Yet, a preoccupation with philosophy from the perspective of experimental science, which was intimately associated with the theory of knowledge, depended on the tools of language to implement both discovery and expression. As the extension and even translation of man's conceptual and perceptual faculties, as the tool ultimately responsible for fashioning what was considered a necessary similarity between nature and a faithful, transcribable image with which both the experimenter and the interpreter would work, language becomes perhaps the single most important element in the attempt to register and to represent "nature's" own independent image (ch. 4). Richard Rorty, in fact, locates the notion of epistemology as itself a consequence of a particular problematics of representation. From its inception in the seventeenth century, "the idea of a theory of knowledge grew up around the problem of knowing whether our inner representations were accurate" (*Philosophy and the Mirror of Nature*, p. 139).

The question of accuracy in our "inner representations" of nature's domain poses epistemological problems whose ambiguous resolution constitutes the language and text of Diderot's methodology in *De l'Interprétation de la nature*. Not only an explicit question addressed by the methodology of experimental philosophy, these concerns of representation are generated by and within the text of science and operate in the capacity of a poetics. My endeavor to restore the dimensions of epistemology to Diderot's proposals for experimental science involves an ensuing focus on the principle of nature as textual referent, as image, as a complex weave of descriptive and narrative functions (ch. 4).

In effect, by reinstating the question of representation and, more specifically, the role of the experimenting, narrating and writing subjects with respect to the realm and image of nature in the text of *De l'Interprétation*, new light may be shed on the contradictory reading of this treatise by the traditions of intellectual history and history of science. What initially kindled my interest in this text and what led me to reexamine it outside the boundaries imposed by each of these disciplines was the paradox of their contradicting interpretations. By outlining the disagreement of intellectual history and history of science at crucial places in Diderot's text, contemporary literary criticism is demonstrated to be more than an alternative structure of interpretation. Rather, it is a method able to provide an interdisciplinary emphasis imperative to understanding the complex strategies of representation implicit in the broad implications of this "predisciplinary" text. The contemporary critic rediscovers the intersections of the human sciences as they were posed in eighteenth-century experimental science through models which are once again less concerned with defining a discipline than with the discourse that of necessity moves between and beyond them.

Across the nineteenth and twentieth centuries' traditional demarcations of philosophy, science, language theory and epistemology, Diderot's *De l'Interprétation de la nature* formulates an image of nature through the strategic textual positioning of a referent, which issue is explicitly at stake in the debates on language theory—debates contemporary with the publication of *De l'Interprétation*. Furthermore, his *Lettre sur les sourds et muets* brings the relation between epistemological criteria and language theory to bear specifically on poetic practice that we have already seen at work in the text on scientific methodology (ch. 5). The epistemological preoccupation with representation constitutes then the point of an isosceles triangle which forms and is formed by the related angles of experimental science and poetics.

Within this context, *Le Rêve de D'Alembert* deals with the coincidence and with the disjunction of science and art, pitting the former against the latter in an attempt to signal a discrepancy become dangerously negligible in Diderot's texts between what is here claimed to be the truly reproductive capability of nascent materialism inherent in nature's structures and the merely imitative capacity of art (ch. 6).

The principle of nature as a textual referent, as image, is charted throughout my study from the perspectives of various subjects such as the experimenter and observer of nature as they are articulated in and by the codes of narration. The concluding pages of this book introduce another external principle, that of painting and sculpture, central to the formulation of Diderot's art criticism in the text of the *Salons.* Already a re-presentation of nature's objects, the referent as it functions in ways similar to its position in *De l'Interprétation de la nature* constitutes a new perspective, one that this study points forward to as the subject of a future book, that is, the conjunction of the natural with the artistic object as textual referent in the "I" of the beholder.

Chapter 1
Text as Document: Document as Text: Why a Poetics of Science?

Il y a donc une bonne et une mauvaise écriture. La bonne et naturelle, l'inscription divine dans le cœur et l'âme; la perverse et artificieuse, la technique, exilée dans l'extériorité du corps. (Jacques Derrida, De la Grammatologie, p. 30)

Studies concerned exclusively with a discussion of Diderot's *De l'Interprétation de la nature* are rare.[1] Yet, every critic of this text situates it at a crucial moment in the evolution of Diderot's thought and, even more emphatically, in the movement of eighteenth-century science and philosophy.[2] In this tradition, discussion of the *Interprétation* usually has taken the form of individual chapters in works which attempt a comprehensive view of enlightenment science and philosophy. Frequently, quotations, even the title, have been extracted from this treatise to illustrate either another work of Diderot or a designated theme of the period.[3] *De l'Interprétation de la nature* has functioned

---

1. *Denis Diderot, "De l'Interprétation de la nature," Œuvres philosophiques,* ed. P. Vernière (Paris: Garnier, 1964), pp. 165-245. Reference to Diderot's text will be made according to this edition and in the text of this study according to fragment and page number. Other editions when necessary will be cited in the notes. The title of the second edition of Diderot's text, published in 1754, *Les Pensées sur l'Interprétation de la nature* will sometimes appear as it is cited in the texts of other scholars.
2. Herbert Dieckmann, "The Influence of Francis Bacon on Diderot's *Interprétation de la nature," Romanic Review,* XXXIV, 1943, and "The First Edition of Diderot's *Pensées sur l'Interprétation," Isis,* X, 1955. With the exception of the above articles and those few reviews written in the eighteenth century as a response to Diderot's *Interprétation* there are almost no other single pieces devoted exclusively to this text. As concerns the reaction to this text of Diderot in the years immediately following its publication, see *Œuvres philosophiques,* Vernière, p. 173.
3. Herbert Dieckmann, "Système et Interprétation," *Cinq Leçons sur Diderot* (Paris: Droz, 1959), pp. 41-68. In this article, Dieckmann uses a concept of interpretation parallel to Diderot's text of the same title as a central focal point and as a paradigm for the discussion of a necessary critical perspective on the thought of Diderot.

for its critics, then, as an example, as an index of a movement which is larger and more encompassing than the essay itself.

In *The Philosophy of the Enlightenment*, Ernst Cassirer cites Diderot's *De l'Interprétation* as a prime example of a major turning point in eighteenth-century scientific inquiry. Citing "fragment III" of this work, which asserts that mathematics is after all only another metaphysical argument, Cassirer states:

> With this observation the ideal of mathematical natural science, which dominated all eighteenth-century physics, begins to fade; and in its place a new ideal arises, the demand for a purely descriptive science of nature. Diderot had grasped and described this ideal in its general outlines long before it was realized in detail.[4]

Further on, Cassirer places Diderot's discovery in the still broader context of a comparison between centuries.[5] And at the end of his chapter On "Nature and Natural Science," Cassirer once more invokes a passage of the *Interprétation* as an illustration of the dynamics of Diderot's thought which, in turn, functions emblematically in Cassirer's text as herald of the "new order of things," of the changes taking place in eighteenth-century studies of philosophy and nature:

> "A new order of things is born" (rerum novus nascitur ordo), the motto by which Diderot characterizes nature, also applies to Diderot's own position in the history of eighteenth-century thought. He introduces a new order of ideas: he not only goes beyond previous achievements, but he changes the very forms of thought which had made these achievements possible and given them permanence. (Cassirer, p. 92)

In his biographical study, *Diderot: The Testing Years*, Wilson attributes to the *Interprétation* the same relevance for the development

---

4. Ernst Cassirer, *The Philosophy of the Enlightenment*, trans. Koelln and Pettegrove (Princeton: Princeton University Press, 1951), pp. 74-75.
5. Ibid., p. 75.

of the author's thought that Cassirer gave it for the development of eighteenth-century philosophical thought as a whole. Referring to the *Interprétation* as a work which is "one of the most important and least read," Wilson assigns to this work the merits of being "one of the ways in which the philosophe proved himself a philosopher."[6]

Wilson links Diderot's treatise, as did Cassirer, with attitudes "characteristic of the point of view of the whole eighteenth century. One of these attitudes is the distrust of elaborate and comprehensive philosophical systems" (Wilson, p. 191). The other was "to regard reason more as an instrumentality than a thing in itself" (ibid.). Lefèbvre declares along the same lines that "l'importance des *Pensées sur l'Interprétation de la nature* dans l'histoire de la philosophie des sciences, de la science elle-même, et de la pensée humaine, ne saurait être surestimée."[7]

As herald of a "new order of things," Diderot's text has functioned critically as both event and document of an event in the history of science and in the history of ideas. Within these contexts, it remains only a seeming contradiction that a work which "ne saurait être surestimée" should receive such limited critical examination. In effect, the very insistence on its extreme importance lies in direct proportion to the repeated inscription of this work within a broader framework. *De l'Interprétation de la nature* stands out as a prominent document to the extent that it has been incorporated into a smooth, linear continuum of history. This history narrates in retrospect the steady progress of western civilization toward its realization in the age of modern science and thought, locating the enlightenment of the eighteenth century at the threshold.

---

6. Arthur M. Wilson, *Diderot: The Testing Years 1712-1759* (New York: Oxford University Press, 1957), p. 187.

7. Henri Lefèbvre, *Diderot*, série Hier et Aujourd'hui (Paris: Editions Réunies, 1949), p. 153. Lefèbvre, in his turn, quotes Jean Luc: "Seul peut-être M. J. Luc a redressé les torts des historiens et mis à sa place ce texte de premier plan, en écrivant que *les Pensées sur l'Interprétation de la nature* sont 'le discours de la méthode du XVIIIième siecle.' " Jean Luc, *Diderot* (Paris: Editions Sociales Internationales, 1938), p. 107.

Inquiry of the past 20 years into historical methodology has attempted to reverse the above pattern of event and document inscribed within a linear chronology of rational progress. Michel Foucault among others has challenged the coherence of this seamless context, calling into question the very notion of history as a linear continuum of cause and effect:

> Sous les grandes continuités de la pensée, sous les manifestations massives et homogènes d'un esprit ou d'une mentalité collective, sous le devenir têtu d'une science s'acharnant à exister et à s'achever dès son commencement, sous la persistance d'un genre, d'une forme, d'une discipline, d'une activité théorique, on cherche maintenant à détecter l'incidence des interruptions.[8]

According to such an argument, the individual document celebrated formerly as a monument to the past recalled by collective memory takes on different attributes. Foucault attempts to liberate these documents from the assumed integrity of a past culture and from an unproblematic relation to the present:

> Il était un temps où l'archéologie, comme discipline des monuments muets, des traces inertes, des objets sans contexte et des choses laissées par le passé, tendait à l'histoire, ne prenait sens que par la restitution d'un discours historique: on pourrait dire, en jouant un peu sur les mots, que l'histoire de nos jours, tend à l'archéologie—à la description intrinsèque du monument. (Foucault, *L'Archéologie du savoir*, p. 15)

The perspectives which have dominated study of *De l'Interprétation de la nature* have indeed exemplified the tendency to make sense of it as a document, indeed, to formulate the notion of document, by explicating it exclusively according to a particular historical discourse and perspective always larger and more encompassing than the text itself. Upon examination, the inadequacy of these methods in pro-

---

8. Michel Foucault, *L'Archéologie du Savoir* (Paris: Seuil, 1969), pp. 10-11.

viding for the complexities of Diderot's text will illustrate the consequent need for another method to ascertain the importance of *De l'Interprétation* and to uncover the unresolved questions it poses. Studies by two representative scholars, Jacques Roger, the historian of science, and Franco Venturi, the intellectual historian, will be demonstrated to justify Foucault's challenge to the superimposition of historical continuity on a past document. My reading of Roger and Venturi, despite their avowed intentions, relocates Diderot's text within the intricate web of associations and contradictions to date glossed over, suppressed.[9]

Any discussion of valid criteria for an understanding of Diderot's treatise must involve its liberation from a tradition which smooths over the rough edges of the text into a coherent historical thesis; the critic must deal with the proliferation of opposing interpretations to which it has given rise. Such a situation is owing to more than varying historical predispositions. Diderot's text engenders what appears to be significations which consistently exceed the limits imposed by any given historical framework. From what critical viewpoint the ensuing paradoxes can be more successfully explored will become apparent as *De l'Interprétation de la nature*, following Foucault's metaphor, assumes the shape of a monument, broken off, separated from its integral cultural, historical context and thereby restored to the status of discontinuity, of fragment—the 58 fragments which in fact constitute the text.

My choice of Roger and Venturi as representatives of previous historical criticism is occasioned by two considerations: firstly, as other critics in their respective disciplines, they tend to determine the central focus of Diderot's treatise according to the concerns of their own disciplines. Roger's point of departure in the history of the natural

9. Jacques Roger, *Les Sciences de la vie dans la Pensée française du XVIIIième siècle* (Paris: Colin, 1963), pp. 585-682. All references to Roger's book will be indicated by author's name and page number in my text. Franco Venturi, *La Jeunesse de Diderot: de 1713 à 1753*, trans. Juliette Bertrand (Paris: Skira, 1939), pp. 283-316. All references to this work will be similarly indicated.

sciences predisposes him to view the central concern of the *Interpréta-tion* as scientific and ultimately speculative in kind. Venturi, as an intellectual historian, discerns the utilitarian aspect of Diderot's treatise in promoting the spirit of the Enlightenment as its primary emphasis. These two extremes can be construed as the poles between which most of the previous criticism has oscillated.

According to Roger, Diderot's interest in the natural sciences, resulting in part from the intellectual milieu of his time, is augmented by a predisposition of temperament to the "réel sensible":

> *Les Pensées de l'Interprétation de la nature* sont donc le résultat de la première rencontre sérieuse de Diderot et des sciences biologiques. Cette rencontre est doublement nécessaire. D'abord parce que la pensée de la première moitié du siècle avait si bien lié les problèmes qu'on pouvait difficilement concevoir une réflexion philosophique qui se désinteressat des sciences de la nature. D'autre part, le tempérament de Diderot répugne aux spéculations abstraites. Sa vision métaphysique de l'univers ne peut se passer des *données concrètes* de la science, pas plus que sa méditation sur l'homme ou sur l'art ne peut ignorer la réalité vécue des sentiments ou des émotions esthétiques. Le recours au *réel sensible* est toujours la démarche la plus spontanée chez Diderot. Du déisme sentimental au matérialisme scientifique, il y a évolution d'une pensée, mais permanence d'un tempérament. (Roger, pp. 612-13)

Such a predisposition coincides with Diderot's major emphasis in *De l'Interprétation* on empirical science to the detriment of mathematics and the abstractions of rationalist speculation. Following in the footsteps of Buffon, Diderot valorizes the life sciences of biology and chemistry in the activities of observation and experimentation. Yet, no sooner posited as fundamental to the study of nature, Roger must qualify the empirical orientation of Diderot's thought. The observer of nature as well as the experimenter cede in importance to the interpreter of nature and subsequently to the exigencies of philosophy and metaphysics. The "manœuvrier," though an essential component in scientific study, ultimately does not rise above the undistinguished rank of worker. Without his contribution, science would remain a series of idle abstractions; but without the interpretation, indeed, speculation of the philosopher, observations would remain merely useless data. Using a comparison with Buffon, Roger insists on Diderot's impatience with a method unable to answer the larger questions concerning the order of things, concerning the "why" as opposed to the "how" of their existence. If for Diderot "la métaphysique doit s'appuyer sur les résultats de la science sous peine de n'être plus que méditation creuse des subtilités de l'ontologie" (Roger, p. 601), Roger also underscores the inverse movement: "C'est qu'il voit dans la science un moyen et non une fin en soi, c'est qu'il lui demande une *connaissance réelle* de la nature, et non un point relatif à l'homme et à son action sur les choses" (Roger, p. 606, my emphasis).

Within this context, what does "connaissance réelle" signify? In contrast to the use of "real" employed earlier to denote man's contact with a nature palpable and knowable through the senses, "le réel sensible," here the term "connaissance réelle" refers precisely to what is posited beyond both man's direct experience and his particular circumscribed perspective. The "real" seems here to be synonymous with a notion of absolute knowledge that resides with metaphysics. Roger's own text swings back and forth between the poles of science and philosophy as they are juxtaposed in Diderot's text, privileging now the "manœuvrier" and observer of nature as opposed to the speculative philosopher, now the interpreter of nature to the detriment of the diligent but limited worker. Man's needs in the present are displaced by the higher activity of science dedicated to the ends of metaphysics and yet, at the same time, Roger insists that Diderot's tendency remains to "tout ramener à l'homme" (Roger, p. 613). Diderot manifests, on the one hand, a commitment to "concrete givens" of science and to the "réel sensible" as the basis for a science of nature, on the other, the scientist's reaction to material data is merely a step that leads away from the present of observation to the importance of interpretation and to the conjectures that reach beyond the observer and experimenter, ultimately surpassing by their questions projecting into the future even the vision of the philosopher.

If this is an accurate account of the movement discernible in

Diderot's text, Roger seems undisturbed by the paradoxes implied with respect to a methodology of empirical science. At what point and moment is the experimenter's role superseded by the role of the interpreter? Where do questions of a metaphysical nature take over, perhaps disrupting the grounds so carefully laid down by a methodology of experimental science? Roger signals an opposition in Diderot's text to utilitarian and empirical science and, in so doing, he displaces problems perhaps too delicate to broach in favor of the other extreme. The potential opposition to an empirical science which *De l'Interprétation de la nature* is supposed, on the contrary, to celebrate is glossed over by Roger's insistence on the less detrimental thesis of Diderot's disdain for the purely utilitarian value of scientific investigation. Roger strings together a series of quotations drawn from a few fragments in the *Interprétation* that scorn the general public for its narrow and self-interested bias in favor of the "utile."

> C'est qu'il voit dans la science un moyen et non une fin en soi, c'est qu'il lui demande une *connaissance réelle* de la nature, et non un point relatif à l'homme et à son action sur les choses. L'utilité pratique de la science apparaît ici comme une nécessité à laquelle Diderot se résigne sans joie: "L'utilité circonscrit tout," constate-t-il (fr. VI). Pour survivre, la science devrait travailler "à la recherche et à la perfection des arts, qu'on jetterait au peuple pour lui apprendre à respecter la philosophie" (fr. XVIII). (Roger, p. 606, my emphasis)

As further proof of Diderot's inclination to speculative philosophy as opposed to any utilitarian approach to science, Roger turns to the series of 15 questions at the end of the *Interprétation*.[10] Roger compares Buffon's acceptance of "le caractère relatif de la connaissance" with Diderot's orientation:

> Diderot ne saurait admettre ce relativisme; il ne pourrait pas davantage s'enfermer dans le présent: il a besoin de savoir ce que sont les choses,

---

10. *Interprétation*, pp. 240-244.

d'où vient l'ordre, s'il est immuable. Les questions qui terminent *Pensées sur l'Interprétation de la nature* trahissent cette impatience: elles exigent une réponse. La réponse viendra 15 ans plus tard, avec *Le Rêve de D'Alembert*. (Roger, p. 614)

Indeed, the questions at the end of the *Interprétation* insist on evoking problems of the most speculative nature. Yet, how they relate to the main body of the text remains to be answered. In fact, the last paragraph of the *Interprétation* relegates these questions explicitly to the background and to the dreams of the scientist. Though he does not renounce them, Diderot situates such speculation in a context, on one level, beyond the scope of man's research, his "bien être" (well-being), and his "civilization."

Quand je tourne mes regards sur les travaux des hommes et que je vois des villes bâties de toutes parts, tous les éléments employés, des langues fixées, des peuples policés, des ports construits, les mers traversées, la terre et les cieux mesurés; le monde me paraît bien vieux. Lorsque je trouve les hommes incertains sur les premiers principes de la médecine et de l'agriculture, sur les propriétés des substances les plus communes, sur la connaissance des maladies dont ils sont affligées, sur la taille des arbres, sur la forme de la charrue, la terre ne me paraît habitée que d'hier. Et si les hommes étaient sages, ils se livreraient *enfin* à des recherches relatives à leur *bien-être* et ne répondraient à mes questions futiles que dans mille ans au plus tôt; ou peut-être même, considérant sans cesse le peu d'étendue qu'ils occupent dans l'espace et dans la durée, ils ne daigneraient jamais y répondre. (*Interprétation*, p. 244, my emphasis)

This very passage, or rather part of it, serves Venturi as proof of Diderot's abiding concern for the mechanical arts, for science as a tool used to benefit society.[11] The shift in critical criteria from the life

---

11. This is the passage as Venturi quotes it (p. 298): "Lorsque je trouve les hommes incertains sur les premiers principes de la médecine et de l'agriculture, sur les propriétés

sciences and their link with philosophy to the social ideals of the Enlightenment leads to the opposition of one interpretation with another. If Roger ignores the last paragraph of the text which follows immediately on the 15 conjectures, so Venturi ignores the 15 questions crucial to Roger, as well as other indices contrary to his perspective. Venturi's quotation of the last paragraph also bears scrutiny because it is incomplete and taken out of context.

The two studies of Roger and Venturi are in direct opposition to one another at the same time that they are complementary. For each presents a partially convincing case by means of quotations drawn from the text to support an argument. Yet, each historian has selected his material by ignoring what the other has emphasized. The extreme partiality of each view is demonstrated and clearly brought into focus by the other's perspective. Once the barrier that holds counter-evidence in check is removed, the reader must come to terms with the complexity of Diderot's thought as it is implied in the apparent contradictory assertions of the *Interprétation* and as it is echoed in the confrontation between Roger's and Venturi's assessments.

Venturi leaves aside both the first part of the quotation referring to the already civilized world, to that which has already been constructed, and the last part of the quotation referring to the series of questions to be answered only in the distant future. He begins his citation with "Lorsque je trouve. . ." and ends at "Et si les hommes étaient sages, ils se livreraient enfin à des recherches relatives à leur bien-être." Extracted by Venturi from its original context, "bien-être" no longer suggests a contrast with the accomplishments of civilization. Yet, in the light of the entire fragment, "bien-être" has broader and more contradictory connotations, signifying man's well-being as deriving less from the benefits of his already civilized world than from investigation

---

des substances les plus communes, sur la connaissance des maladies dont ils sont affligés, sur la taille des arbres, sur la forme de la charrue, la terre ne me paraît habitée que d'hier. Et si les hommes étaient sages, ils se livreraient enfin à des recherches relatives à leur bien-être" (*Interprétation*, p. 244).

into the still unknown "first principles" underlying man's sophisticated accomplishments.

On one level, "bien-être," as it is situated in Diderot's passage, appears to signify a decidedly material situation that permits man to satisfy the needs of his existence. In this capacity, "well-being" clearly contrasts with what Diderot himself termed the "futile" philosophical speculation of his conjectures. Yet, in the light of the passage's initial contrast, such a uniform reading is baffled and the term "bien-être," losing clear temporal and spatial reference, defies a literal reading. The first section of this passage is conceived in terms of a correlation between society's progress and man's age. Whereas the built-up cities and ports along with social structures such as language seem to establish man's maturity, and whereas all natural elements of the earth, sea and air have been domesticated to social use and structure, the uncertainty concerning knowledge of "first principles" of agriculture and medicine, along with persisting ignorance surrounding the principles and operations of society's tools and most elemental substances, reveal man to be still near infancy. It is in enjoining man to pursue answers to these fundamental questions that Diderot contrasts "bien-être" with the futility of speculation. Thus, the adverb "enfin" appears to place man on sure ground where he can reap the material benefits of his accomplishments; yet, his well-being is posited in a time still to be established and in a space as yet undefined by the parameters of his seemingly sophisticated constructions.

As quoted by Venturi, "bien-être" is made to assume positive connotations as contrasted with the negative of purely speculative questions. But this term as situated in the text is highly metaphorical and in so becoming breaks its literal link with the notion of man's material existence, which on the other hand this term seems exclusively to signify. "Bien-être" is related in the text to knowledge of first principles of medicine and agriculture as opposed to the enjoyments or the benefits of the same, or as opposed to the further sophistication of technique in the various fields mentioned. Diderot gives concrete expression to an enterprise and to a concept which are explicitly extended beyond the literal and specifically empirical connotations implied.

The qualitative change Diderot marks with "enfin" is precisely an investigation into "first" or underlying principles. Speculation is limited supposedly to questions of present usefulness with regard to established disciplines of science. Yet, how can one answer questions concerning the first principles of medicine and agriculture without knowing, without raising questions about, "les propriétés des substances les plus communes," and without eventually, or soon, raising the very questions about the origin of life made explicit in the 15 conjectures preceding this final fragment? In other words, calling for men who are wise to occupy themselves with their "bien-être" seems in this fragment only apparently in opposition to scientific and philosophic speculation. A closer look reveals that the concept of "bien-être" is made to fulfill ultimately contradictory objectives.

Venturi, nevertheless, makes specific use of this passage to illustrate Diderot's position in the "polémique des lumières" as a

> combattant pour une science *claire* mais *utile*. L'idée des limites que la société pose à tout cycle de connaissance se fond avec cette hostilité à l'esprit de système qui est caractéristique du XVIIIe siècle pour faire de Diderot le héraut d'une connaissance utile au bonheur de l'homme. (Venturi, pp. 297-98, Venturi's emphasis)

It is following the above statement that the controversial passage is situated in Venturi's commentary. The orientation toward a knowledge bringing "bonheur" to society is reinforced in the same part of Venturi's chapter on the *Interprétation* by his insistence on Diderot's desire to render science available to the general public: "C'est qu'il y a dans tout l'écrit que nous examinons une volonté nettement proclamée de rendre la science populaire et de la mettre à la portée de tous, qui n'est pas l'un des aspects les moins intéressants de cette période de la pensée de Diderot" (Venturi, p. 297). Clearly, Venturi and Roger are essentially at antipodes.

The adjectives "utile" and/or "pratique" appear consistently throughout Venturi's analysis of Diderot's text and are crucial to this critic's overall interpretation. Already from an initial statement in the preface, the reader is informed as to the scope of Venturi's study in terms congruent with the above stated notion of a "science utile." Venturi points out that criticism has long struggled vainly to situate Diderot's thought with regard to a specific philosophical content. The result has too often been to judge Diderot's work as incoherent, even to qualify Diderot as "incapable de se concentrer et de nous donner une grande œuvre" (Venturi, p. 7):

> Et pourtant, le chef d'œuvre de Diderot existe; il a plus de vingt volumes in-folio et son titre a donné son nom à une école et à une époque: *l'Encyclopédie.* . . . Ce n'est certes pas une œuvre philoso-phique, ni artistique: c'est un chef d'œuvre *pratique.* (Venturi, p. 8, my emphasis)

The attribute "pratique" in the above quote situates the *Encyclopédie* as a cornerstone of a historical process in which political and social reality are transformed. Diderot's *Encyclopédie* is crucial, according to Venturi, to the change that took place from the first to the second half of the eighteenth century. From primarily literary and/or religious works written in the first half of the century a new animation is realized through:

> un enthousiasme, une énergie, une force suffisante pour faire de la France le centre d'une Europe conquise aux lumières. Or, Diderot est l'un des artisans de ce changement, l'une des forces essentielles qui amenèrent cette insertion des idées et des rêves des philosophes des lumières dans l'histoire de la France et de l'Europe. (Venturi, p. 9)

The "dreams" of the *philosophes* come to life in a "force" which Venturi translates into "la politique" responsible for changing Europe as a whole: "Voir la naissance, dans l'âme de Diderot, de cette nouvelle force, tel est le but de cette étude" (Venturi, p. 10). This historian admits a perspective from which the ideas of Diderot are considered "plutôt dans leur efficacité et dans leur raison du moment que dans leurs origines philosophiques" (ibid.). Venturi translates Diderot's texts into social, political forces whose significance is located less within the content of a particular work than in the spirit of European society.

In his study of the *Interprétation*, Venturi locates the conjectures and dreams of the philosopher within a realm situated beyond human dimension. Yet, this critic simultaneously relegates just this process to an historical efficacity and to a social utility. Venturi draws a series of parallels between the attributes ascribed by Diderot to the movement of nature's cycles, those cycles inherent, according to Venturi, in the development of the various sciences and their instruments, and those qualities such as intuition intrinsic to the genius of experimental science.[12] The attribute "pratique" is used to modify both "intuition" and "creation." A question is already raised by the union of terms potentially disparate if not antithetical. Both "l'intuition pratique du génie" and "la création pratique de l'humanité" are, regardless of their attendant adjectives, presented by Venturi as exceeding the practical. In effect, Venturi emphasizes that aspect of genius which is "plus obscure et plus fécond" than any particular intellectual tool such as analogy (Venturi, p. 286). Furthermore, Venturi illustrates the way in which the creations of science and of the arts follow a movement modeled on that of nature. Man can neither recognize the true origin of a specific machine or object, nor can he imagine its creation before its actual appearance: "Il arrive qu'on ne puisse définir un produit en tant qu'il est le résultat d'une certaine machine. Les hommes d'avant n'eussent même pas pu l'imaginer" (Venturi, p. 295).[13]

---

12. Venturi, pp. 287-88.

13. Man's products follow the same course as nature's species:

(a) "La nécessité qui guide le développement d'un organe, qui fait qu'un être vivant s'adapte aux conditions environnantes, c'est la nécessité même qui guide l'homme dans toutes ses créations." (Venturi, p. 289)

(b) "Et même que les espèces vivantes, les sciences ont leur cycle de vie, lequel se borne à leur utilité sociale, c'est-à-dire, en somme, à leur vitalité au sein de la société humaine." (Venturi, p. 289)

(c) "Une fois que tout ce processus d'adaptation s'est produit, l'instrument créé par le 'génie' de l'homme rentre, pour ainsi dire, dans la nature. Il devient aussi simple que pourrait l'être un produit de la nature même." (Venturi, p. 295)

"Practical," as Venturi uses the term, does not qualify the interpreter's "intuition" or "creation" with respect to the immediate spatial or temporal spheres of activity where they function but with respect to the ultimate, tangible consequences and products of these activities— not as precedent to or productive of, but as the ultimate *effects* of intuition and creation. In his comprehensive parallel established between science and genius, on the one hand, and the transformational movement of nature, on the other, Venturi takes the conjecture, termed "rêverie" in the earlier 1753 edition of the *Interprétation*, to the ultimate stage of an already palpable, accomplished reality, seeing the passage without interruption and without paradox.[14]

Venturi does not assess the individual work *De l'Interprétation* according to the coherence of a philosophical or scientific system or methodology as proposed within Diderot's text. He does bestow a coherence on Diderot's text by insisting on its ultimate influence in the domain of the methodology of science according to the text's position within the linear movement of history. Just as, according to Venturi, the process of experimentation and discovery defined in the *Interprétation* is based on the larger process of nature's revolutions and productions, so the importance of the text itself is to be measured by the larger, comprehensive and uninterrupted process of civilization's scientific and intellectual progress.

The parallel effected by Venturi between the individual text or discovery and the larger movement of nature and history implicitly depends, therefore, upon a necessary gap that must prevail between nature's process and man's endeavors, between the intention of the scientist or author and a particular subsequent result or interpretation, between individual experimentation and collective discovery. Man's

---

14. "Conjectures" termed "rêveries" in the first edition of the *Interprétation* were introduced in the following manner: "Car j'appellerai une Rêverie ce que d'autres nommeroient peut-être un système," *De l'Interprétation de la nature* (Paris, 1753), p. 73. The title of the work was also changed in 1754 to *Pensées sur l'Interprétation de la nature*.

techniques and inventions become relevant when integrated into a broader scope and chronology, when they are separated from the immediate context of his intentions and endeavors. Yet, it is to Diderot's writing as the product of an individual consciousness that Venturi refers in his praise of Diderot's works. If the merits of *De l'Interprétation* are attributed by Venturi to a dynamics that is constituted specifically beyond an individual subject as organizing principle, Diderot's treatise on the methodology of science, like the texts of the *Encyclopédie*, is nevertheless posited as an originary moment, and one in which the intentions of the author are exchanged for the nebulous but more metaphysically expansive concept of the "soul": "Voir la naissance dans l'âme de Diderot, de cette nouvelle force, tel est le but de cette étude" (Venturi, p. 10).[15]

Venturi's work exemplifies a historical study that recuperates the past by positing a series of origins to be located within a totalizing movement of scientific and intellectual progress. As Diderot projects man's answer to the problems of the "first principles" of science and philosophy into a future situated beyond the scope of a lifetime, even of generations to come, so Venturi gives form to these "dreams" by locating them in retrospect as the origin of what was to follow and of what was with hindsight to be realized.

Under the polished surface that a history of ideas and a history of science would impose on the *Interprétation*, the polyvalence of certain critical and textual terms tends nevertheless to undermine the stability of the traditional discourse imposed. The history of science and the history of ideas oppose each other through the medium of Diderot's text and within each discipline *De l'Interprétation de la nature* evokes a difference, a discrepancy. History of science as the point of departure in Roger's work must accommodate metaphysical speculation as an

---

15. Foucault locates the emphasis on "origins" within the perspective of traditional history: "Faire de l'analyse historique le discours du continu et faire de la conscience humaine le sujet originaire de tout devenir et de tout pratique, ce sont deux faces d'un même système de pensée. Le temps est conçu en termes de totalisation et les révolutions n'y sont jamais que des prises de conscience." (Foucault, *Archéologie*, p. 22)

integral aspect of Diderot's experimental methodology just as Venturi's perspective of intellectual history validates Diderot's ideas inasmuch as they are translated with hindsight into the practical utility of social progress.

As Venturi has employed it, the term "pratique" works in two modes in its application to Diderot's text: as a function of nature, "pratique" defines the interpreter's intuition and genius as they parallel and even participate in the process of nature; at the same time, "pratique" is also ascribed to the results and benefits of such a movement in terms of a broad historical scope where the effects and results of genius and intuition are measurable eventually in terms of social utility. The avowedly impalpable and unfathomable forces of intuition and genius are reconciled, then, with the pragmatism celebrated in Venturi's notion of social utility. Yet, both poles of this seeming antithesis are contaminated by their opposite, so that social utility takes on broader connotations that do not exclude the limitless designs of man's scientific and philosophic queries, while intuition and genius, if assimilated into the cycles of nature itself, are also inscribed within the parameters of practical social benefits.

Any reading of the connotations implied in Diderot's use of "bien-être" involves the recognition of its fundamental ambivalence. For while the passage in question contrasts the notion of society's well-being with "futile" speculation concerning the visible results of civilization's accomplishments, the practical exigencies of man's well-being exceed the limits of his immediate needs, thus pointing to the necessity of speculative philosophy. Fulfilling seemingly contradictory functions, the term operates as a pole to mathematics and to the negative qualities of abstract science on the one hand; on the other, it is assimilated in Roger's text to speculative questions which would concern a knowledge of "first principles."

The above methods and disciplines appear to compound the problems involved in reading *De l'Interprétation de la nature* by echoing unaware the text's ambiguities. The terms employed by scholars to encompass this polyvalence, as in the case of Venturi's use of "pratique" or Roger's "connaissance réelle," play down the opposition between the realm of the pragmatic and theoretical while at the same time they prolong or extend such ambivalence within the fixed framework imposed by the discipline in question. At stake in the oscillation between the speculative and the practical are not only the demarcations to be established or, rather, to be traversed between science and philosophy but those boundaries between the literary/non-literary text, between the text whose value lies in its reference to the objects of knowledge translatable into certain codes by a metalanguage and the text whose value lies precisely in its resistance to such an operation.

The need to reevaluate the criteria of diverse literary genres and the varying discourses of the human sciences with respect not to their content but to differences in the function of language has been keenly felt in the past 20 years by formalists, structuralists and post-structuralists alike. The excess of signification we have identified in Diderot's text, which generates diametrically opposed historical interpretations, is related to problems posed by a critic such as Roman Jakobson in his concept of "surdétermination." This term is central to Jakobson's inquiry into the nature of literary as opposed to non-literary language. For Jakobson, the term "surdétermination" defines a language "de haute teneur sémantique," applicable to literature and especially to poetry.[16] Because of their originality of style, their subject matter conceived as primarily non-referential to extra-linguistic entities, literature

---

16. Roman Jakobson, "Qu'est-ce que la Poésie," *Questions de poétique* (Paris: Seuil, 1973), p. 124: "Mais comment la poéticité se manifeste-t-elle? En ceci, que le mot est ressenti comme mot et non comme simple substitut de l'objet nommé ni comme explosion d'émotion. En ceci, que les mots et leur syntaxe, leur signification, leur forme externe et interne ne sont pas des indices indifférents de la réalité, mais possèdent leur propre poids et leur propre valeur." Speaking of the problems of translation in another essay, Jakobson says: "La poésie par définition, est intraduisible." *Essais linguistiques* trad. française (Paris: Minuit, 1963), p. 86. Translation is the basis for both Jakobson and for Emile Benveniste of the concept of metalanguage: "La faculté de parler une langue donnée implique celle de parler de cette langue. Ce genre d'opérations 'métalinguistiques' permet de réviser et de redéfinir le vocabulaire employé" (Jakobson, ibid., p. 81). See also Benveniste, *Problèmes de linguistique générale*, vol. II (Paris: Gallimard, 1967), p. 65.

and particularly poetry can neither be paraphrased nor translated without an ensuing loss to the inherent qualities of their language.

A "cognitive text," on the other hand, allows, necessitates translation and paraphrase into established codes such as, precisely, the codes supplied by the history of science or the history of ideas. A loss of value in the case of literary or poetic texts can be contrasted with the positive value of paraphrase or translation in cognitive texts "qui visent à se construire et à se proposer comme lisibles, textes pédagogiques ou encyclopédiques qui tendent à s'échanger contre un gain de contenu, de savoir, d'information."[17]

Yet, viewed critically in its potential function as a "cognitive text," Diderot's treatise provides both more and less than the traditional spheres of intellectual history or history of science can accommodate. This excess reverses the rule of exchange, cancelling the putative "gain" to be derived from a paraphrase or translation of the work. Such recoding does not bring clarification or necessarily additional knowledge but tends to disrupt and to confound the categories of the metalanguage applied to the text. Should not Diderot's *Interprétation* be studied as a literary text, then, rather than as a non-literary cognitive document? How does the language of Diderot's *Interprétation* signify?

This tendency of modern critical thought to concentrate on the signifying practices and structures of language without regard to the boundaries and delimitations of disciplines or genres echoes the preoccupations of the eighteenth century. To put it in a way more congenial to an eighteenth-century perspective on science and philosophy, language was considered integral to knowledge and played a major role in all epistemological queries of the *philosophes.* Diderot's treatise, as this book will demonstrate, provides an example of the manner in which language was considered a repository for devices and strategies used to advance epistemological concerns and, for this very reason, was the object of intense scrutiny by philosophers, grammarians and men of letters alike. Any inquiry into the function of

17. Philippe Hamon, "Métalangage et littérature," *Poétique*, 31 (1977), p. 264.

language in the *Interprétation* is complicated from the start, then, by the implication of language in the thematics of the text itself. A treatise purporting to advance a valid method for the study of natural philosophy was by necessity during this predisciplinary phase of the human sciences obliged to consider as well as to enact the theories and strategies of language fashioning and subtending the interpreter's relation to nature.[18]

In effect, the changing focus of modern critical and theoretical orientation has increasingly uncovered an emphasis in the eighteenth century itself on the interplay of theories of natural history, experimental physics, philosophy and science with the theory of language. An intimate association of knowledge and epistemology with language theory was already playing an essential role in philosophy toward the end of the seventeenth century in the work of John Locke, whose importance to the subsequent French doctrines of sensualism and empiricism has long been an accepted fact.[19]

Several studies point out the fact that Locke's critique of Cartesian innate ideas is associated with an orientation away from speculative philosophy to the physical and empirical sciences and that such reorientation involves a different concept of language:

> La science expérimentale exigeait un nouveau pacte d'alléance entre l'ordre des choses et l'ordre des mots, la recherche de la vérité doit se

---

18. Wilda C. Anderson makes a useful distinction between the *philosophes'* "predisciplinary attitude" toward knowledge in the eighteenth century and the modern "interdisciplinary attitude" in *Between the Library and the Laboratory: The Language of Chemistry in Eighteenth-Century France* (Baltimore: Johns Hopkins University Press, 1984), p. 4.

19. For Hans Aarsleff (*From Locke to Saussure: Essays on the Study of Language and Intellectual History* [Minneapolis: University of Minnesota Press, 1982]), "the important consequence is especially that with Locke's *Essay* laying the foundations of the modern study of languages, the origins of this study become tightly intertwined with the major intellectual event in our centuries, the rise of the new science in the seventeenth century. This fact permits language study to gain its rightful place in intellectual history" (p. 27).

borner à transcrire la réalité des faits tels qu'ils s'offrent à l'investigation objective et contrôlable.[20]

From Locke's description of language in his *Essay*, we learn that words, understood as arbitrary conventions, are conceived as technical implements which can be adequately perfected to describe the physical realm: "Le langage n'est qu'une description du réel; la voie empirique seule subsiste pour l'enrichissement du savoir; la correction du langage ira de pair avec la correction de la connaissance" (Gusdorf, p. 290). Locke emphasizes the possibility of perfecting a language which in its adequation with the physical realm will finally achieve an objective knowledge through description:

> And therefore, in substances, we are not always to rest in the ordinary complex idea commonly received as the signification of that word, but must go a little further and inquire into the nature and properties of the things themselves, and thereby perfect as much as we can, our ideas of their distinct species.[21]

"Words," as understood in the above quote, inasmuch as they represent individual ideas, must first be distinguished and separated from substances and objects as they exist in nature. Knowledge of substances in nature is not contained in the words, names, in the language that heretofore have designated them. Locke develops a theory in which words as arbitrary conventions should function primarily as references to extra-linguistic reality. According to Hans Aarsleff, Locke was, in effect, the founder of modern language study in that he realized the necessity for a semiotics based on the principle of words as

20. Georges Gusdorf, *L'Avènement des sciences humaines au siècle des lumières* (Paris: Payot, 1973), p. 290. See also David Givner, "Scientific Preconceptions in Locke's Philosophy of Language," *Journal of the History of Ideas*, vol. XXIII (1962), p. 340.

21. John Locke, ed. Alexander C. Fraser, *An Essay Concerning Human Understanding* (New York: Dover, 1959), II, 161.

arbitrary conventions.[22] Locke took a position that contrasted sharply
with any notion of a natural or Adamic language in which the word
participates in the secrets and in the reality of objects. "Locke's view of
language was entirely functional."[23] As a series of conventions that can
be perfected in order to achieve an accurate description of the natural
world, language as a purely functional tool must be differentiated
from the subjective perceptions which not only differ from one
individual to another with respect to the understanding of a particular
linguistic term, but which prevent study of objects or substances in
and for themselves.

> By this means it comes to pass that men speaking the language of their
> country, i.e. according to grammar rules of that language, do yet speak
> very improperly of things themselves; and, by their arguing one with
> another, make but small progress in the discoveries of useful truths, and
> the knowledge of things, as they are to be found in themselves, and not
> in our imaginations. (Locke, II, 162).[24]

In fact, the notion of subjective perception and representation, when
related to language, is consistently intimated in Locke's text to be
located on the other side of authoritative, referential description.

We might go a step further here to say that in these passages, Locke
endows language with the potential for referring to "things in themselves" by designating nature in this passage as an external realm, that
is, as different and separate from the individual's perceptions, mental
operations and language which represent it. The rhetorical strategy
employed here conveys the idea of the independence of nature's realm

---

22. Aarsleff, *From Locke to Saussure*, pp. 27-29.
23. *Ibid.*, p. 28.
24. Here is another example of the division between subjective thought and the
nature of "real essences" given by Locke: "What then, are we to do for the improve-
ment of our knowledge in substantial things? Here we are to take a quite contrary
course: the want of ideas of their real essences sends us from our own thoughts to the
things themselves as they exist" (Locke, *Essay*, II, 348).

by means of a discrepancy pointed up between the perspective of an individual subject and what lies beyond him and which the tool of language must translate. As opposed to a domain where individuals contest their own understanding of an entity or substance, language must become a series of neutral implements used to identify and describe nature. Every thinker, every speaker then would relate to language in the study of nature in a new way, as a medium specifically not appropriable as his own.

Diderot did not fully share Locke's view on perfecting language to perform as so many arbitrary conventions employed to describe the natural world. As an extreme example of a language of signs, devoid of any relation either to the individual who wields them or to the referent they quantitatively define, mathematics is viewed throughout the *Interprétation* as useless precisely because of its fundamentally arbitrary values and therefore because of its ultimately metaphysical argument. For Diderot, the term "metaphysical" implies a series of formulae which in their inability to approximate, to resemble the domain of nature, seem so many "jeux," or arbitrary conventions (fr. III, p. 179). Language as code, as a series of symbols, is exactly the medium and approach Diderot deems it so important to avoid. Yet, if Diderot endeavors to substitute for mathematics a method and a language of science neither arbitrary nor purely conventional, what is the relation between language and the physical world? Is language to partake of nature? Is language to pass then from *techne*, from artifice, to an imitative or natural language? What would this imply concerning a study of nature from the perspective of a language geared to accommodate empiricism and an experimental method?

Nonetheless, in a move reminiscent of Locke, we will see that Diderot's *De l'Interprétation de la nature* also posits nature's objects in contradistinction to the individual philosopher's ideas and terms. The same necessary dichotomy obtains throughout the text between an external realm of nature to be described and investigated and the individual's own conceptions, as was the case with Locke. But here, it is in the name of the preconceptions inherent in the rationalist system, and rejected by Diderot as so many abstractions indiscriminately applied to nature's objects, that a dichotomy takes shape in the *Interprétation* between what Diderot terms the traditional rationalist philosophy and the new method of experimental philosophy. And it will be in the name of a language conceived very differently from that of a semiotic system that the relation between the interpreter and the object of his investigation will be recounted.

If one considers, first, that experimental philosophy is related to the sensualist doctrine's positing of a feeling, experiencing subject in direct response to the stimuli which first occasion an awareness of the world and, secondly, that at the same time the Cartesian model also posits a subject—a thinking subject, the cogito—but as the principle from which all knowledge ultimately derives, prior to any consideration of extended matter or of nature's attributes, then we can begin to conceive of the complexity involved in the positioning of the experimenting, investigating subject in *De l'Interprétation de la nature*. For while these subjective entities appear to occupy contrasting positions in their respective orders, both sensualist and Cartesian doctrines endow the subjective principle with a primary role; both are identifiable in language and in the text as the first-person. Diderot's treatise has been understood as a step in the opposite direction to that taken by Descartes' deductive method, and toward a new method which would take account of empirical data gleaned from nature prior to positing any scientific and, particularly, metaphysical system, thereby denying the precedence of the cogito; on the other hand, the importance of such a feeling, experiencing subject as a receptacle, as an entity constituted by perceptual response and by nature's attributes, also necessitates the presence of the individual subject to delineate in and through language an external frame of reference.

In other words, the scientific and philosophical project of *De l'Interprétation de la nature* is defined and constituted in this text to a great extent by the particular mode of representing the individual investigating and interpreting subject. The role of the subject in the language of the *Interprétation* is crucial and integral as well to the project of the narrator as a writing subject whose discourse is part of the rhetorical strategy essential to conveying, indeed to articulating, a philosophical position. So, in one sense, Diderot carries on the tradition established by Descartes, in which the philosopher builds his argument and constructs his method on his own experience in the first-person of autobiographical writing. *De l'Interprétation de la nature* demonstrates its filiation to the *Discours de la méthode* at the same time that the autobiographical project of the writing subject is in fact subverted.[25]

Chapter II explores the investigative strategy of Diderot's protagonist, the experimenter, the interpreter of nature. Here, as we discussed earlier, the apparent contradictory functions of language will be studied with respect to the strategic positioning of a subject as organizing principle in the text. The very movement of separation created to ensure a spatial delimitation and a temporal deferral of the writing and interpreting subject with respect to the realm of nature's objects is doubled by a mimetic movement that works to locate and to found these subjects within the natural process. The interpreter speaks about a nature constituted by physical entities and simultaneously speaks from, speaks as, this nature. Hence, as implied in this treatise, Diderot's view of language exceeds Locke's emphasis on the referential or implemental value of words, when they are posited as deriving meaning from an implicit and "original" connection to things.

Chapter III of this study reveals the textual strategies invoked by Diderot to displace the origin of an idea or observation to a space and time external and precedent to that of the writing subject. Diderot's empirical tenets can be correlated with a separation marked out in the text between the subject as narrator or as experimental scientist and a nature that is positioned through language so as to exist independently of and prior to these same subjects as organizing principles. The

---

25. For an analysis of autobiography in Descartes' *Discours de la méthode* in specific relation to epistemological concerns, see Wilda Anderson, *Between the Library and the Laboratory*, pp. 6-13. For an interesting notion of Descartes' construction of the self in spatial terms, see Jean-Joseph Goux, "Descartes et la perspective," *L'Esprit Créateur*, XXV, 1 (Spring 1985): 10-21.

writing subject situated in the *Interprétation* will bear comparison to a form of autobiography prevailing in French eighteenth-century fiction, that of the memoir novel. Discussion of similar devices employed in this genre to situate a protagonist who is also the writing subject with respect to his/her own life experiences will help to highlight an epistemological concern predominant in the language and rhetorical devices that constitute experimental philosophy and fiction.

The representation of things, of the physical realm in the imagery of the *Interprétation*—entities posited in language but suggesting an exteriority to it—, expands the dynamics of the narrating, interpreting subject. Chapter IV discusses the recurrent textual pattern that subordinates a discursive element of a passage to the descriptive, pictorial image. The opposition word/object is carried out in these passages by means of a distinction between two levels of language: discourse and image, and between the representation of two registers of thought: linear and simultaneous. Now the position of the subject as organizing principle of both thought and language is, not coincidentally, placed into question in the debates on "inversion" during the 1750's and 1760's. This French polemic waged by grammarians and *philosophes* focused precisely on the relation of subject to object within the syntactic order of sentence structure. An examination in chapter IV of the opposing sides as to the correct and/or most persuasive order of French syntax reveals in paradigmatic manner the philosophic, esthetic, as well as linguistic issues at stake in the textual manœuvres of *De l'Interprétation de la nature.* Moreover, the existence of two distinct points of view in this question corresponds to the double movement at work in Diderot's text. For the implications of the two positions with respect to "inversion"—language as primarily referential and conventional, and language as natural and mimetic—are both involved in Diderot's poetics of science in the *Interprétation*. Diderot took an active part in this debate; chapter V explores the issue of "inversion" as it is addressed in *Lettre sur les sourds et muets*. Not surprisingly, Diderot's response in this work does not coincide exclusively with either position but corroborates his double approach to language as illustrated by *De l'Interprétation*.

My final chapter studies Diderot's textual representations of nature in the context of *Le Rêve de D'Alembert*. In its capacity of science, materialism is contrasted in Diderot's text to metaphysical speculation, on the one hand, and to the art of statuary and fiction, on the other. While the art of sculpture is judged severely as a mere copy of nature, the materialist experiment as recounted in the text is assimilated to the process of nature. This chapter will demonstrate how, as in the work of Diderot studied in earlier chapters, nature is sought as an external, concrete principle on which the narrative, on which the enunciating speaker, is made to depend. Yet, in laying bare the linguistic devices employed to formulate the metaphor of nature, the rhetorical function of language will be seen to undo even as it constructs the myth of a "natural" language, a text of nature.

From a treatise on the methodology of experimental philosophy to contemporary eighteenth-century constructs of fiction, to theories of language advanced in contemporary documents, our reading will criss-cross disciplines and genres in the wake of Diderot's hybrid discourse to determine the place of the subject as an organizing epistemological principle of these texts, as an esthetic criterion and as a poetic perspective. Yet, by nature of its integral role in reestablishing the importance of language to Diderot's scientific, philosophical project, the problematic aspect of the discoursing, writing, experimenting subject becomes apparent. For the particular emphasis in the text on the principle of a subjective perspective is represented so as to negate its importance, to obscure if not to deny its precedence. In other words, to represent the writing, discoursing, experimenting subject as always dependent on something other than and prior to its own activity in language marks its very rhetorical capacity as well as its ambiguity. In a historical sense, our study documents a moment when the subject, having become the locus of a paradox, is on the brink of disappearing altogether from its representation in the text of science and philosophy, where language will be increasingly relegated to a domain uncontaminated by the mark, the autograph or the place of the subject. Because of the divorce between science and literature, between literature and philosophy, which Barthes situates as already evolving since the sixteenth century,[26] Diderot's work demonstrates what has been, before the advent of modern criticism, unthinkable: that a methodology proclaiming the necessity of experimental science as a vehicle for true knowledge of nature's object world is wrought from the very rhetorical structures that such methodology precludes.

Before Nietzsche, recognized as one of the first modern thinkers to have addressed the fundamentally mystifying quality of language taken as truth, Diderot's texts grant an awareness that

The paradigmatic structure of language is rhetorical rather than representational or expressive of a referential, proper meaning. This marks a full reversal of established priorities which traditionally root the authority of language in its adequation to an extra-linguistic referent or meaning, rather than in the intra-linguistic resources of a figure.[27]

As this book attempts to illustrate and as they have worked in other and perhaps more surreptitious ways in subsequent texts, the metaphors of nature, of the self and the subject are employed throughout Diderot's *De l'Interprétation de la nature* in the service of a poetics that founds the representational authority of a language of science.

26. Roland Barthes, "De la Science à la littérature," *Times Literary Supplement* (1967), repr. in Barthes, *Le Bruissement de la langue* (Paris: Seuil, 1984), p. 14.

27. Paul de Man, "Nietzsche's Theory of Rhetoric," *Symposium*, vols. 28-29 (1974-75), p. 35.

Chapter II
The Poetics of Diderot's Interpreter: The Hero and His Properties

Le soleil ne donne pas seulement un exemple, fût-il remarquable entre tous, de l'être sensible en tant qu'il peut toujours disparaître, se dérober au regard, n'être pas présent. L'opposition même du paraître et du disparaître. . . , du jour et de la nuit, du visible et de l'invisible, du présent et de l'absent, tout cela n'est possible que sous le soleil. Celui-ci, en tant qu'il structure l'espace métaphorique de la philosophie, représente le naturel de la langue philosophique. (Derrida, *Marges de la philosophie*, p. 299)

. . . la philosophie rationnelle . . . dit hardiment: *on ne peut décomposer la lumière*: la philosophie expérimentale l'écoute, et se tait devant elle pendant des siècles entiers; puis tout à coup elle montre le prisme, et dit: *la lumière se décompose*. (Diderot, *De l'Interprétation*, p. 193)

Science, like literature, has its heroes. The genius celebrated by society for his/her discoveries in the physical or mathematical realm has also at moments been portrayed as a specific persona within the text of a scientific treatise. The relation of such a figure to the particular methodology advanced in Diderot's *De l'Interprétation de la nature* is a question this chapter will explore. Just as the study of any protagonist in a novel ultimately involves the narrative technique as well as the thematics and the language which structure this representation of a protagonist, so a study of the experimental scientist as he is characterized in the work of Diderot's treatise will shed light on broader questions of scientific methodology—on Diderot's poetics of science and on the ways language participates in the enterprise of experimental philosophy.

Diderot's treatise particularly lends itself to such an analysis in his portrayal of "l'interprète de la nature."[1] For, as opposed to the neutrality and highly technical style with which the scientific treatise has increasingly come to be identified, Diderot's work is concerned with a broad spectrum of questions as defined by the general category of "physique expérimentale," and its language is as yet undefined by a specialized or technical field. What appears to organize this methodological treatise is the scientist, or, to use Diderot's term, "le génie expérimental," whose privileged perspective dominates the activity of interpretation. If central to the concept of interpretation as it is posited in Diderot's treatise, the "experimental genius" can nevertheless consistently be seen to participate in what might be termed "excentric" activity.

Since the publication in 1753 of Diderot's work, Francis Bacon has been considered a precursor and in some instances a direct model for Diderot's treatise.[2] As is commonly known, *De l'Interprétation de la nature* echoes the title employed by Bacon in three of his works and is a term to which he frequently has recourse throughout his writing.[3] In an article directed toward clarifying the similarities and differences of theory and methodology in the work of these two authors, Herbert Dieckmann introduces a contrast pertinent to our analysis here. According to this scholar, Bacon not only hesitates before the idea of

---

1. *De l'Interprétation de la nature*, fr. LVI, pp. 234-35. I will discuss this fragment at length as well as others which have bearing on the notion of the interpreter, sometimes termed a "génie de la science expérimentale" (fr. XXX, pp. 196-97). Herbert Dieckmann specifically links the "interprète" with the "génie" so that "we seem to have in the interpreter of nature the scientist Diderot expected for the new investigation of things outlined in the *Interprétation*" ("The Influence of Francis Bacon on Diderot's *Interprétation de la nature*," *Romanic Review*, vol. 34 [1943], pp. 324-25).

2. For a discussion of criticism which cites Bacon's influence on Diderot's *Interprétation*, see Dieckmann, ibid., pp. 303-04.

3. "Interpretation of nature" is not only a fundamental theme of Bacon's thought and a term occurring frequently in his writing, it is also the title or subtitle of three of his major works: *Cogitata et Visa de Interpretatione Naturae; Novum Organum, sive Indicia Vera De Visa de Interpretatione Naturae; Valerius Terminus, De Interpretatione Naturae*.

"conjecture" essential to the procedure of "le génie expérimentale," he does not develop a notion of the privileged perspective of the scientist who penetrates nature where others do not: "the notion of an individual endowed with specific insight into nature can not be found in Bacon" (Dieckmann, p. 316).

The differences in those works of Diderot and Bacon which transform the position of the experimental scientist and genius within each methodology form, in fact, a clear symmetry as yet unnoticed by critics and which will bring into sharp focus the relation of Diderot's protagonist to the textual patterns of *De l'Interprétation*. The outline of this opposition can be stated in the following manner: method and theory dominate in Bacon's notion of interpretation, whereas for Diderot the privileged scientist-subject is rendered as an enactment of interpretation to the detriment of a rigid system of method and theory.

Though in certain instances in Bacon's work the scientist is indeed endowed with the dimensions of a specific mythological or historical-epic hero, the portrayal of such figures exist in the text outside of and extrinsic to the elaboration of method and experimentation.[4] Bacon's notion of "interpretation" centers on the description of a method, on the discovery of forms by means of induction, whereas Diderot concentrates on the individual "interprète" of privileged insight. A symmetry is created then by the specific locus of the subject within these two operations. Curiously enough, however, the very terms of this initial dichotomy—Bacon positing method as the principal structuring element, Diderot insisting on the importance of a particular insightful individual—are reversed in chiasmatic fashion with respect to the nature of both the method and individual defined: Bacon's emphasis in his theory of the method of induction falls on a controlling, fully

---

4. Within the context of the European heroic tradition, John M. Steadman points out "Bacon's eulogy of the experimental scientist as heroic benefactor, founder, discoverer, conquerer; an exemplar not only of heroic wisdom but of heroic charity" ("Beyond Hercules: Bacon and the Scientist as Hero," *Studies in the Literary Imagination*, IV [1971-74], p. 5).

aware consciousness operating at the center of experimentation; inversely for Diderot, this process is described as taking place explicitly and necessarily beyond the subject's full awareness and control, even, as we shall see, beyond sense perception itself.

Neither chance nor inspiration, neither special insight nor divination, working in Diderot's portrayal of the "interprète," is valorized by Bacon who relegates "mere experience" to chance and to a position of inferiority:

> Science will progress only if experience is directed by a fixed law and made in regular order, i.e. if methodological research replaces the simple gathering of experience and trusting to chance. (Dieckmann, p. 313)

The place of the subject can be best understood initially then as a function of these two authors' differences concerning experimentation as chance or controlled method. A comparison of some crucial passages will best illustrate and develop this complementary opposition.

After enumerating and discarding ways unfruitful for man's acquisition of knowledge, Bacon comes to a distinction between "mere experience" and "experiment": "There remains but mere experience, which, when it offers itself, is called chance; when it is sought after, experiment."[5] The purposeful "sought after" as opposed to "offers

---

5. "Novum Organum," *The Works of Francis Bacon*, ed. James Spedding, R. L. Ellis, D. D. Heath (London: Longmans and Co., 1857-74), "Philosophical Works," I, 231-539; VIII, 59-350. Reference to Bacon's *Novum Organum* will be made according to this edition in both Latin and English. Here is the full Latin quote to be discussed in the following pages: "Restat experientia mera, quae, si occurrat, casus; si quaesita sit, experimentum nominatur. Hoc autem experientiae genus nihil aliud est, quam (quod aiunt) scopae dissolutae, et mera palpatio, quali homines noctu utuntur, omnia pertentando, si forte in rectam viam incidere detur; quibus molto satius et consultius foret diem praestolari, aut lumen accendere, et deinceps viam inire. At contra, verus experientiae ordo primo lumen accendit, deindre per lumen iter demonstrat, incipiendo ab experientia ordinata et digesta, et minime praepostera aut erratica, atque ex ea educando axiomata, atque ex axiomatibus constitutis rurus experimenta nova; quum nec verbum divinum in rerum massam absque ordine operatum sit" (I, 289).

itself" (*si quaesita sit/si occurrat*), is a term which structures the opposition in the description that follows:

> But the true method of experience on the contrary first lights the candle, and then by means of the candle shows the way; commencing as it does with experience duly ordered and digested, not bungling or erratic, and from it educing axioms, and from established axioms again new experiments; even as it was not without order and method that the divine word operated on the created mass. (*Novum Organum*, LXXXII, vol. VIII, p. 115)

Though active in terms of its semantic value, "sought after" remains an impersonal verb—indicative of the description of procedure that follows. For that which sets up the light, and also "shows the road by it," is of course the "true method of experience" (*At contra, verus experientiae ordo primo lumen accendit, deindre per lumen iter demonstrat*). On the grammatical level, method occupies in this sentence the position of subject. This subject precedes and controls grammatically just as, on a conceptual level, method organizes and comes before to ensure and control the due order of method. Such a tautology can be seen precisely as a function of the concentration on method to the detriment of a designated controlling human agent and persona. In such a formulation, the persistent use of active verbs underscores a series of procedures rather than individual actions, articulated around an absent human agent or rather, in "lighting the candle" (*lumen accendit*) and "showing the way" (*per lumen iter demonstrat*), the true order of method has the textual value of a personified theory.

The light, which metaphorically "shows the road by it" and therefore precedes the experiments or axioms to be essayed, guarantees by its sign the correctness of direction, is itself the visible effect of the "true" method, and also provides the cause for the initial direction of experimentation. Such metaphorical light contrasts with darkness ascribed by Bacon to "mere experience" as chance:

> But this kind of experience is no better than a broom without a band, as

the saying is;—a mere groping, as of men in the dark, that feel all around them for the chance of finding their way; when they had much better wait for daylight, or light a candle, and then go. (*Novum Organum*, LXXXII, vol. VIII, p. 115)

The opposition between day and night, light and darkness accompanies that between the explicit introduction of man as subject of "mere experience," one without center or aim and, as shown above, the substitution of the "real order of experience" for the human subject. In fact, the above quotation refers to man in a negative capacity, on the occasion of his blind errors. This comes in the passage directly before, and stands in sharp contrast to ordered experience as the new and more successful agent (the Latin uses the strong expression "At contra"). Nonetheless, such "real order of experience" explicitly performs, indeed better, all the tasks of an organizing principle.[6]

Diderot's portrayal of experimental science as well as his description of the "génie expérimental" adopt a set of parallel and contrasting oppositions between light and darkness. In what appears to be almost a direct response to the above passage from Bacon, Diderot declares the light, the "torch" of "rational science," to be inferior in its results to the blind groping of experimental science:

6. In this context, it is interesting to consider Wilda Anderson's rigorous discussion of Descarte's rhetorical strategy in the *Discours de la méthode*. Anderson first identifies a "circular proof" operating in the *Discours* by means of an argument using "logic to support experiential events and the description of those events to support the authority of logic" (Anderson, p. 10). In this way, Descartes can propose a "natural method," one "he did not have to think up himself" (Anderson, ibid.). Moreover, "the author of any statement, from this point on, appears to be the method itself, and the authority that stands behind it is God" (Ibid., p. 11). Already before Descartes, Bacon's strategy illustrates a similar move to exchange method for man's individual fallibility. The difference is that this new authority of method in Bacon's text does not have to be separated as is the case with Descartes from the autobiographical writing subject. According to Anderson, "the relationship of authority and authorship has been dismantled" (Anderson, p. 11). See my chapter III for Diderot's use of autobiographical writing with respect to method and to the interpreter of nature.

Nous avons distingué deux sortes de philosophies, l'expérimentale et la rationnelle. L'une a ses yeux bandés, marche toujours en tâtonnant, saisit tout ce qui lui tombe sous les mains, et rencontre à la fin des choses précieuses. L'autre receuille ces matières précieuses et tâche de s'en former un flambeau; mais ce flambeau prétendu lui a, jusqu'à présent, moins servi que le tâtonnement à sa rivale et, cela devait être. (*Interprétation*, fr. XXIII, pp. 192-93).

Diderot's passage ascribes inverse values to light and darkness. Darkness, employed by Bacon as a conventional metaphor for man's intellectual inability to see and to understand, in other words, for the lack of a prescribed order and method, signifies for Diderot a place of hidden, unknown but appropriable treasure. Accordingly, the notion of chance is also weighted differently by the two authors: for Diderot, chance discovery positions the experimenting subject as receiver of precious material and information; for Bacon, chance, or what he terms "mere experience," deprives the scientist of a fully aware pursuit and order of knowledge. So, though Diderot's "génie" initially organizes the activity of interpretation, this activity itself is consistently portrayed as taking place outside the boundaries of a rigorously defined methodology as well as beyond the coherence and integrity of the scientist-subject centrally posited at the outset. Darkness for Diderot conveys the passive state of the experimentalist receiving stimuli, stumbling upon things, upon truth, whose existence is guaranteed as real precisely because not preconceived. Unlike Bacon's use of the metaphor of darkness, employed to depict human fallibility, a state of mind uncorrected by method and order, absent to nature's truth and divine light, darkness in Diderot's text assumes the function of a metaphor for the depths of the earth, for the material and internal substance of nature itself.

Insistence, therefore, on dark subterranean places finds entry into several fragments of the *Interprétation*. And this underground movement is ultimately subversive; it is shown to dismantle the very foundations of the rational construct:

Mais le temps a renversé jusqu'aujourd'hui presque tous les édifices de la philosophie rationnelle. Le manœuvre poudreux apporte tôt ou tard, des souterrains où il creuse en aveugle, le morceau fatal à cette architecture élevée à force de tête; elle s'écroule. . . . (*Interprétation*, fr. XXI, pp. 191-92)

The opposition between a purely intellectual construct easily toppled and the concrete if always fragmented pieces of experimental proof is constituted by the elaboration of the experimenter's physical approximation to the process of nature, depicted in spatial terms as hidden and secret places where the precious treasures of discovery are continually to be found and experienced. The underground activity of digging, of descending into the earth, places emphasis on process to the detriment of an inflexible stasis inherent in the constructs of abstract systems created by ungrounded and preordained calculations of method and order. The researcher loses himself to nature's workings without predetermined or preconceived design, in imitation of nature's own otherwise unfathomable process; this mimetic gesture always entails in the *Interprétation* the renunciation of a fully aware controlling principle of experiment.

Representation of the individual experimenter as organizing center of this "excentric" process of interpretation takes the shape of a short story recounted in two consecutive fragments of Diderot's text. A dying father relates the whereabouts of a hidden treasure to his sons, the protagonists of the tale; an ensuing search enacts the interpreter's state of awareness in terms of the opposition light/darkness, above/below the earth's surface. On instruction from their father, the sons set out with the specific purpose of locating "un trésor caché dans son champ": "ils ne trouvèrent pas le trésor qu'ils cherchaient; mais ils firent dans la saison une récolte abondante à laquelle ils ne s'attendaient pas" (*Interprétation*, fr. XXVIII, p. 196). The presupposed existence of glittering treasure gives way to the product of the earth's substance and abundance, a good harvest. Most importantly, the expectations of the sons are baffled in that what does come as a boon is totally unexpected. In this allegory of research and experimentation, the position of the interpreter and "manœuvrier" with respect to their avowed project and to their desire is persistently displaced in order to accommodate the "real" events and objects of nature.

A second fragment continues the story for a repeat performance. The following year, the sons attempt once again to gain access to the buried treasure, with similar results:

> Nous nous sommes assurés, par notre travail de l'année passée, que le trésor n'est point à la surface de la terre; il faut donc qu'il soit caché dans ses entrailles; prenons incessamment la bêche, et creusons jusqu'à ce que nous soyons parvenus au souterrain de l'avarice. (*Interprétation*, fr. XXIX, p. 196)

A more explicit emphasis in this fragment on the subterranean depths of the earth is accompanied by a further opposition between the glitter, the brilliance of treasure and the lead mine which, nonetheless, as in the first year, yields unexpected riches:

> Ils avaient déjà creusé profondément sans rien trouver; l'espérance commençait à les abandonner et le murmure à se faire entendre, lorsqu'un d'entre eux s'imagina reconnaître la présence d'une mine, à quelques particules brillantes. C'en était, en effet, une de plomb qu'on avait anciennement exploitée, qu'ils travaillèrent et qui leur produisit beaucoup. (*Interprétation*, fr. XXIX, p. 196)

These avid brothers, bent on becoming rich, must first bend over their shovels towards the earth before appropriating its bounty. With this fragment, as with the preceding one, a discrepancy between what they seek and what they find is constituted by the difference between a product of avarice which is also artifice, buried treasure crafted and manipulated by man, and those riches integral to nature's own production. Both a good harvest and a lead mine need man's endeavors to be brought to fruition, but both exist already as potential inherent in nature. The contrasting light and darkness continue to operate in the sequel to the story where further descent into the entrails of the earth becomes necessary and where the expected brilliance of gems, like the alchemist's long-awaited dream of gold, turns into the dull, opaquely sombre element of lead. All attributes of lead, its position in and of the earth's deepest recesses, its transformation from initial brilliance in the mine to dull gray once exposed to air, emphasize in terms of the substance itself a proximity and even resemblance to the earth that produced it.[7]

The resources of experimental science for Bacon are represented in an allegory where the true order of method and theory are personified as the fixed subject controlling experiment. It is this personification that structures the contrast of darkness and light as metaphors portraying the state of mind of knowledge or ignorance. A particular state of mind is informed by typical metaphors used to distinguish the presence or absence of knowledge. The "natural" attributes of the sun in its relation to the earth are assimilated into man's philosophical constructs while man's role in the process of seeking, of determining knowledge, is reduced in Bacon's text to a seemingly disembodied theory of method. In Diderot's reworking of Bacon's thesis on experimentation as the basis for knowledge, more is at stake than a new emphasis on the role of the experimenter's privileged insight that supersedes a concept of ordered method. Diderot's reelaboration of the opposition between darkness and light, between blindness and insight, is structured by a different concept and a different function of metaphor—one that will play an increasing role in the following pages as it also figures throughout the *philosophe*'s writing.

The fragments where the experimenting subject gropes blindly in the dust and dirt of the earth's deepest recesses restructure the traditional use of light/darkness by relating the attributes of darkness to the

7. The article "Plomb" in the *Encyclopedie* (vol. XII) describes lead as one of the heaviest metals: "C'est d'après l'or, le mercure, et la platine, le corps le plus pesant de la terre." When first seen in the earth, it will often be "d'un blanc bleuâtre fort brillant, lorsqu'il a été fraîchement coupé, mais qui devient d'un gris mât lorsqu'il est resté longtemps exposé à l'air." As for lead mines, they are "plus riches à mesure qu'ils s'enfoncent profondément en terre."

earth, thereby valorizing the processes or dynamics of nature's hidden operations. Not only are traditional pejorative connotations of darkness inverted into the positive connotations of nature's material substantive reality, the quality of the earth's objects and movements take on consistency by dint of their difference from man's "clear," "enlightened" and abstract constructs. But the earth's physical properties, the dark color of its soil and depth, qualify the place where the experimenter must penetrate and are extended to define the experimenter's blind groping as he participates in, or rather, as he becomes *a part* of nature's own unfathomable workings.

This metonymical chain, which through the attributes of darkness links a literal description of earth's color, density and depth to the place of the experimenter's investigation, also metaphorically links his ignorance, absence of conscious method and predetermined perspective to the dynamics of nature's material reality. The attributes of human ignorance have thus been conflated with the unknowable—earth's mysteries—which is also the all-knowing. Metaphor and metonymy then become the essential tools representing a science and a method that purport to go beyond the organized perspective of a superimposed system, order and language. The experimenter's ignorance is assimilated through the rhetorical devices of language to the absence of definable perspective inherent in the true dynamics of material nature.

The perspective generated by this context situates the experimenting, interpreting subject on the margins of the distinction between ignorance and genius, between dispersion of the interpreting subject in imitation of nature's process and the effect of nature's difference from a finite human perspective. Fragment XXX, immediately following the story of buried treasure, specifically addresses the "genius" of experimental science in terms of the qualities of inspiration and divination. The "démon familier de Socrate" is summoned on an analogy with the process of interpretation. According to principles observed in the above fragments, there is a shift in perspective from the reasoning philosopher as controlling subject to the subject as passive to what lies outside and external to his presuppositions:

La grande habitude de faire des expériences donne aux manœuvriers d'opération les plus grossiers un pressentiment qui a le caractère de l'inspiration. Il ne tiendrait qu'à eux de s'y tromper comme Socrate, et de l'appeler un "démon familier." Socrate avait une si prodigieuse habitude de considérer les hommes et de peser les circonstances, que dans les occasions les plus délicates, il s'exécutait secrètement en lui une combinaison prompte et juste, suivie d'un pronostic dont l'événement ne s'écartait guère. (*Interprétation*, fr. XXX, pp. 196-97)

Socrates' ability to judge men and circumstances is attributable not to his fully aware conscious resources but to a "démon familier." This repeats our earlier example of a displacement of a controlling subject to a position excentric to his own faculties, to his own action. And the thematic transposition is emphasized by an accompanying grammatical shift in the subject of the sentence from "Socrate" as ostensible agent of the action and of the act of judging to an impersonal "il" of the reflexive verb, "il s'exécutait." Such a shift functions to usurp the active role of the philosopher, rendering him a container, a vessel in which the activity carries itself out. The entity of Socrates is relegated to a position of reliance on another force which enters, specifically without his knowledge or control, "secrètement en lui."

The same mechanism is reiterated at the end of this fragment. Speaking of those whose genius allows them to penetrate nature where others do not, Diderot sketchily alludes to a plan for the instruction of other would-be experimental scientists:

Ainsi le service le plus important qu'ils aient à rendre à ceux qu'ils initient à la philosophie expérimentale, c'est bien moins de les instruire du procédé et du résultat, que de faire passer en eux cet esprit de divination par lequel on *subodore*, pour ainsi dire, des procédés inconnus, des expériences nouvelles, des résultats ignorés. (*Interprétation*, fr. XXX, p. 197, Diderot's emphasis)

The adjectives "inconnus," "nouvelles," and "ignorés," all concur to denote the ability of the experimentalist to seize what lies beyond his presuppositions and to react to what lies external to his own knowledge ("résultats ignorés").

A comparison in fragment LVI of the "interprète" with the "observateur" of nature more fully develops the process which engages the experimentalist's privileged perspective:

> L'esprit épouvanté de ces progrès à l'infini des causes les plus faibles et des effets les plus légers ne se refuse pas à cette supposition et à quelques autres de la même espèce que par le préjugé qu'il ne se passe rien au delà de la portée de nos sens, et que tout cesse où nous ne voyons plus; mais une des principales différences de l'observateur de la nature et de son interprète, c'est que celui-ci part du point où les sens et les instruments abandonnent l'autre; il conjecture par ce qui est, ce qui doit être encore. (*Interprétation*, fr. LVI, p. 235)

Initially, this passage seems to provide the reader with all the attributes expected by now of the experimental scientist, and more specifically, of nature's "interpreter." The activity of the conjecturing interpreter is anticipated in an allusion to those less endowed who entertain a "préjugé qu'il ne se passe rien au delà de la portée de nos sens, et que tout cesse où nous ne voyons plus." The light which for Bacon must advance systematically at the same time to generate and to guarantee a valid rational method here remains extinguished. And in its place reigns the darkness emblematic of the interpreter's fruitful groping. Another element recognized as a recurrent strategy in Diderot's description of the interpreter is the use of personal pronouns to define and to delimit boundaries beyond which the subject cannot pass in full awareness and in full control.

As chapter 3 and 4 will elaborate, the use of personal pronouns, in this instance the adjective "nos" and the subject pronoun "nous," allows for a creation of boundaries separating the external world from the realm of the merely subjective. The individual perspective of the interpreter is portrayed in these instances in a manner so as to elicit what lies external to it. In fragment LVI, a positing of the subjective perspective evokes the unfathomable region "où nous ne voyons plus." The darkness of a domain located beyond the controlling force of the individual perspective sets the stage, then, for the appearance of the "interprète."

Under closer scrutiny, however, the first part of this fragment will be seen to suggest a more radical description of the interpreter than is substantiated in the second part. A distinction between the observer of nature and its interpreter is introduced immediately following a mention of unknown regions. Those who are limited, who have prejudged (*préjugé*), remain within the conventions of the senses and of thought refusing to give credence to what lies beyond these confines. Yet, at the place in the text at which the opposing definition of the experimental scientist as interpreter is to be instated, the definition takes a curious turn. At the point the reader awaits an elaboration of a movement through which the interpreter accedes to regions "où nous ne voyons plus," abandoning the conventional realm of the senses, "celui (l'interprète) part du point où les sens et les instruments abandonnent l'autre (l'observateur)."

On the one hand, the above distinction appears less radical than what was initially intimated to be the qualifying gesture of scientific genius. A definition of the interpreter in terms which would portray him as explicitly transgressing the limits of sense perception is exchanged for an emphasis on those limits attributable to the mere observer of nature, "où les sens et les instruments abandonnent l'autre." Consequently, a quantitative difference in individual capacities replaces the initial and more extreme allusion to stepping outside the framework imposed by the normal perceptual and cognitive constitution.

The reason for such a shift in perspective that blurs the outlines of the interpreter results from the lack of a way to refer to or to describe such a privileged perspective and persona except through his difference from the common range of ability and perception. Neither is there a means to evoke the positive content of what is defined as eluding the normal comprehension and perspective; this is witnessed throughout the *Interprétation* in the emphasis on defining the experimental genius with regard to the dark and to an *absence* of clear, logical principles. At the same time, a complete change in registers has been suggested. For the distinction between the observer and the interpreter is elaborated in terms of the very entities, "les sens et les instruments," which in the earlier part of the fragment the interpreter is described as having left behind, as having transgressed.

On the one hand, the interpreter "conjecture par ce qui est, ce qui doit être encore," thereby extending himself "où nous ne voyons plus." On the other, such a leap is immediately qualified: "Il tire de l'ordre des choses des conclusions abstraites et générales, qui ont pour lui toute l'évidence des vérités sensibles et particulières" (fr. LVI, ibid.). These conclusions turn out to have been relegated all along to proofs lent by "vérités sensibles." Moreover, the conjecture entails both an ascension of the interpreter to the essence of an order and, simultaneously, his relegation to ascertainable facts:

> Il s'élève à l'essence même de l'ordre; il voit que la coexistence *pure* et *simple* d'un être sensible et pensant, avec un enchaînement quelconque de causes et d'effets, ne lui suffit pas pour en porter un jugement absolu; il s'arrête là; s'il faisait un pas de plus il sortirait de la nature. (Ibid., Diderot's emphasis)

The text projects the interpreter beyond or above the senses and the resulting scientific data, while subsequently it appears to annul the initial gesture. This double movement is once again discernible in the last sentence of the above quotation.

From his lofty position designated in "il se lève à l'essence même de l'ordre," the interpreter of nature pronounces himself incapable of making a "jugement absolu." More importantly, what he does see from the vantage point of his privileged perspective is his own position, his own predicament. The term "coexistence" refers not only to the relation between "être sensible" and "être pensant"; it alludes to the relation between this complex "être" and "un enchaînement quelconque de causes et d'effets." "Coexistence" has, moreover, a third significance. It alludes to the relation between the perspective of the interpreter and his object of study. In this particular instance, the interpreter seems to be viewing the coexistence of his own thinking and feeling being ("être") with the chain of cause and effect. Separated by the boundaries of commas, this chain does not bridge the gap between "être" and its causes and effects. "Lui" refers directly to its antecedent, "l'être pensant et sensible," as the object under the interpreter's investigation while at the same time "lui" belongs to the interpreting subject himself.

Diderot's text both posits the interpreter outside his own existence as a thinking, feeling being and reinscribes him within the chain of cause and effect he is supposedly tracing. The impossibility of attributing an absolute judgment to what he witnesses is also portrayed within the syntax of the sentence as being an admission of the ambiguity and even inaccessibility of such a privileged perspective: "Il s'arrête là; s'il faisait un pas de plus, il sortirait de la nature." Initially, the interpreter seems to realize a perspective outside of and extrinsic to such relativity of the human condition. Insofar as a thinking and feeling being witnesses a series of causes and effects in strict accordance with his own existence, this must be the extent to which his judgment is from the outset circumscribed.

Yet another index of the shift in perspective away from the more radical positioning of the interpreter can be seen in the evolution of the term "naturelles." Earlier in the fragment, the term *naturelles*, as it appears italicized in the text, signifies tentative and unknowable limits to the dynamic movement of hypothesized molecules:

> Supposez une molécule déplacée, elle ne s'est point déplacée d'elle-même; la cause de son déplacement a une autre cause; celle-ci, une autre, et ainsi de suite, sans qu'on puisse trouver de limites *naturelles* aux causes, dans la durée qui a précédé. Supposez une molécule déplacée, ce déplacement aura un effet, et ainsi de suite, sans qu'on puisse trouver de limites *naturelles* aux effets dans la durée qui suivra. (*Interprétation*, ibid., Diderot's emphasis)

The term "natural limits" with its italicized adjective, *naturelles*, illustrates the ultimate paradox that ensues from an ambiguous positioning of the interpreter "là où nous ne voyons plus." On one level, this fragment conveys the impossibility of superimposing limits on the complete chain of a molecule's displacements: neither can the origin of this movement be traced far enough back in the past, nor can any telos be confirmed. In other words, nature's order and patterns as they are observed and investigated are always displaced with respect to nature itself. Only from a particular perspective, such as that of an interpreter, is the domain of the *natural* created. These displacements of molecules must be studied exclusively in terms of a particular vantage point or perspective that arbitrarily constitutes the realm of nature through its very limits. *Nature*, then, is not *natural* since any individual, human perspective defines conventional limits that arrest nature's dynamics in order to focus on one "frame" of the total picture. Italics, in their function as diacritical marks, set off "nature" as a sphere delimited by any and every human perspective from that domain knowing no boundaries, no end, no representation.

It would appear that this fragment requires the interpreter to define his perspective with regard to recognizing the limits qualifying him as a finite entity. To go further, to pronounce on his conjectures in any "absolute judgment" would be to take up a position and a perspective metaphysical in kind. "Il s'arrête là; s'il faisait un pas de plus il sortirait de la nature" (*Interprétation*, fr. LVI, ibid.).[8] Yet, as this circumscribed

---

8. Dieckmann alludes to the experimentalist's "inexplicable intuitive awareness of the works of nature" (Dieckmann, p. 315), which in Diderot's text has a corollary in "the procedure of nature itself which always follows a rationally obscure, yet nevertheless purposive force" (Dieckmann, pp. 315-16). According to this critic, however, "Diderot never consciously formulated the idea but it underlies his characterization of 'le grand manœuvrier' " (Dieckmann, p. 316). Though the analogy is not explicitly articulated as such, indications such as those shifts sketched in fragment LVI definitely point to an awareness of the dangers involved in extending the interpreter's perspective to that of nature's process. Besides, our analysis shows that no matter what was the author's "conscious" awareness of the analogy between nature and the interpreter's perspective, the text is structured by rhetorical strategies that elaborate this complex relation between nature and the perspective of the interpreter.

frame of reference is set into place, is diacritically imposed in the text, it is against just such a landscape that the portrait of the "génie" must of necessity be drawn.

Diderot's "génie expérimental" is posited also within the boundaries of "nature" at the same time that it is his perspective that occasions its very constitution. In effect, a frame of nature commensurate with the ideals of experimental science and in opposition to the negatively valued implements of mathematical abstraction is shaped not only by the interpreter's existence portrayed as constitutive of the frame but also by the multiple ways in which he is presumed to be situated beyond it. The threat to Diderot's "génie" of stepping outside these limits beyond which he risks becoming confused with an unutterable, undeterminable perspective and language is, nevertheless, the same textual gesture which portrays the "interprète" as dispossessed. Unaccountable to the order imposed exclusively by method, the persona of the interpreter of nature, the experimenter, "le grand manœuvrier" and even the most humble worker ("manœuvrier") endowed with genius, is shaped on his distance from certain possessions, even from his own faculties.

Desire for buried treasure, for property, is not a gratuitous detail in the fragments concerning the two brothers analyzed earlier; it reinforces the thematic emphasis on devices of ownership to be displaced. At moments the interpreter is described as "possessed" by the spirit of genius ("Comment cet esprit se communique-t-il? Il faudrait que celui qui en est possédé descendît en lui-même pour reconnaître distinctement ce que c'est, substituer au démon familier des notions intelligibles et claires, et les développer aux autres" [fr. XXXI, p. 197]). Or he is depicted as beyond reason: "C'est cette habitude de déraison que possèdent dans un degré surprenant ceux qui ont acquis ou qui tiennent de la nature le génie de la physique expérimentale" (*Interprétation*, fr. XXXII, p. 199). To "possess" madness or to be possessed by genius; to be situated outside the realm "où nous voyons"; to be displaced with respect to the faculty of smell (the interpreter who "subodore")—these are the attributes that predominate in the portrayal of the experimental genius. Excentric to his own faculties of sight, of smell, he descends into the earth beyond the conventional markers of property. His very waking state is supplanted by the realm of dreams, fashioned by the "extravagances" of nature: "Je dis *extravagances*; car quel autre nom donner à cet enchaînement de conjectures fondées sur des oppositions ou des ressemblances si éloignées, si imperceptibles, que les rêves d'un malade ne paraissent ni plus bizarres, ni plus décousus?" (*Interprétation*, fr. XXXI, p. 198, Diderot's emphasis).

The organizing subject must be depicted as peripheral, as displaced, from a center that, within each fragment, such movement is creating. Each of these instances represents a discrepancy that functions insistently to separate the experimenting, interpreting subject from his own faculties, his own properties, those particularly which define him as a rational, consciously controlling agent. At stake in this dispersion is a textual strategy whose ostensible aim is to validate the results of discovery.[9] For these fruits of research in experimental science can appear to stem from data gleaned from a material reality that, precisely, is not evoked nor organized in advance as a pre-text for nature.

The representation of Diderot's experimental genius is construed in direct response to an attitude manifested as a prevalent theme in the language of eighteenth-century empirical and physical science: the explicit association of a subjective perspective, of the first-person in discourse, with fiction, with an individual's own biased ideas and

---

9. The term "dispersion" has gained currency in contemporary Diderot criticism. A 1984 bicentennial tribute to Diderot (Jack Undank and Herbert Josephs, eds., *Diderot: Digression and Dispersion* [Lexington: French Forum, 1984]) is organized around this concept by title and in the preface: "Perhaps the dominant impression that is created by the various essays brought together here is one that guides us usefully away from the temptation to view Diderot's 'compulsion' to digression and dispersion as a departure from, fall from or transgression of some fixed center that might possess a prior temporal existence and that is identical to itself always even if nowhere represented" (p. 15). "Dispersion" in the context of the interpreter can be seen to serve specific rhetorical needs.

results, contradictory to what is slowly evolving as history, scientific fact, "objective" knowledge. Throughout many scientific texts of the period, a dichotomy can be traced which locates the subjective pronouns "je," "nous" on the opposite side of verifiable facts pertaining to natural phenomena and process. Locke spoke of a language to be perfected which would name "things as they exist" not as "our imagination" conceives them.[10] Newton's famous "hypotesi non fingo" already merged the subjective perspective with the verb "fingere," to feign, to pretend, ultimately, to fictionalize.

"Hypothesis" as understood in the eighteenth century belongs to the realm of experimental science and to the attempt at gathering empirical data unassimilated by a preconceived system of a philosopher; but to the extent the ordering of data took place not within a certified system but according to the conjectures of a specific individual perspective, it remained specious. Bacon tended to frown on hypothesis, but as late as the publication of *De l'Interprétation de la nature*, so did most theorists and scientists of the time.[11] Within this framework, Diderot's insistence on conjecture and hypothesis was a major innovation.[12] Jean Mayer cites Boureau-Deslandes as a spokesman for current opinion at the time:

A l'égard des hypothèses, quelque bien travaillées et quelque ingénieuses qu'elles soient, on doit en faire le même cas que font des

---

10. Locke, *Essay, op. cit.,* II, 162.

11. "Tandis que des savants comme Musschenbroek ou l'abbé Nollet proscrivaient absolument les hypothèses en sciences, Diderot est à peu près le seul de son époque à les défendre." Jean Mayer, *Diderot, Homme de science* (Paris: Imprimerie Bretonne, 1959), p. 114.

12. "On ne saurait trop insister sur ce point: la méfiance de Diderot à l'égard des systèmes correspond à un esprit d'époque, à une mode. Son originalité, c'est d'avoir conservé à l'hypothèse une place dans la science expérimentale, où il lui fait un role constructif" (Mayer, p. 117). Roger also cites Diderot with reference to the innovation of hypothesis (Roger, *op. cit.,* pp. 603-05).

fables et des romans ceux qui aiment la vérité historique. (Jean Mayer, p. 114).[13]

The analogy that historical truths are to fables and novels as scientific truths are to hypotheses suggests a fundamental opposition between fiction and fact, imagined and external reality. Moreover, it is to the individual's organization and invention that fiction, fables and novels are attributable. "Vérité historique" supposed a collective authorship tantamount to no authorship. "Truths," be they historical or scientific, are considered as representable independent of the artist's hands which fashion them, "ingénieuses" though they may be. The very quality of "genius" then is suspect in its status as highly individual.

The opposition of fiction and fact according to a distinction between what is or is not "propre" to the individual subject finds entry into the eighteenth-century formulation of scientific methodology. Diderot's mentor in the sciences, Buffon, uses this dichotomy in the service of furthering the study of the physical sciences as opposed to the subjective abstractions of mathematics:[14]

Il n'y a rien dans cette science que ce que *nous* y avons mis. . . . ainsi les vérités mathématiques ne sont que les répétitions des définitions ou suppositions. (Buffon, "De la Manière d'étudier et traiter l'histoire naturelle," I, 76-77, my emphasis)

Such a formulation is not uncommon to Buffon nor, as will be shown even more clearly in chapter IV, to Diderot. Again, with regard to Buffon's insistence on the study of the natural world in terms other than mathematical:

13. André François Boureau-Deslandes, *Receuil de différents traités de physique et d'histoire naturelle propre à perfectionner ces deux sciences* (Paris: Quillau, 1748), p. 232.

14. Georges Leclerc de Buffon, *Histoire naturelle générale et particulère, Œuvres complètes* (Paris: Impr. Royale, 1744-1789), vol. I.

Les vérités mathématiques . . . ont l'avantage d'être toujours exactes et démonstratives, mais abstraites, intellectuelles et arbitraires. Les vérités physiques au contraire ne sont nullement arbitraires et ne dépendent pas de *nous*; au lieu d'être fondées sur des suppositions que *nous* avons faites, elles ne sont appuyées que sur des faits. (*Histoire naturelle*, 1ier discours, my emphasis)

Hypothesis or conjecture as well as the experiments on which they are based must ensure, to be considered valid, their adherence to facts. But the definition of facts is often delimited in eighteenth-century texts by their dependence on what lies explicitly beyond manipulation of the controlling subject.

De l'Interprétation de la nature is no exception. Like others at this point in time, Diderot does not rid his discourse on science of the first-person and its markers, of the privileged individual perspective. On the contrary, the rhetorical devices set into play in the *philosophe*'s text give testimony to an elaborate paradox in which this privileged perspective of genius is employed in the service of demarcating, of fashioning a realm, nature, which is other and which informs the genius—not through a chain of cause and effect but through a metonymical chain—with its otherness, its "extravagances."

In his landmark article, "Diderot et la parole des autres," Jean Starobinski examines the interpenetration of Diderot's narrators, of his subjects, with the words of the other: other historical figures, other interlocutors within the text and in the *Rêve de D'Alembert*, with the other of nature.[15] Not only is the question broached: "Mais est-il encore possible de dire 'je' ou 'nous'?" (Starobinski, p. 18), but "l'autre" is ascribed as well to the process of nature. Starobinski is more willing than Poulet to admit that the resolution to this question is not here in a perfect unison which bespeaks a simple integration of individual with other, of reflection with nature.[16] However, Starobin-

15. Jean Starobinski, "Diderot et la parole des autres," *Critique*, 296 (1972), pp. 3-22.
16. Georges Poulet, *Etudes sur le temps humain* (Paris: Plon, 1950), pp. 194-217.

ski confines himself only to the analogy between the two. He does not speak of their possible oppositional and even necessary contradictory relation.

Within the context suggested by Starobinski, *De l'Interprétation* provides a wedge with which we can observe a discrepancy between human reflection and the activity of nature even as, or rather, precisely because, the text works to overcome such difference. Starobinski seems here to ignore that "l'activité de la nature" can only be represented in and as text. If he takes such representation for granted, the complex rhetorical strategies that articulate the position of the experimentalist genius in *De l'Interprétation de la nature* show that Diderot does not.

Perhaps it is easier to understand, then, how Roger and Venturi find corroboration for contrasting readings of the *Interprétation* in certain elements of the same text (see my first chapter). A concept such as man's "bien-être," which for Venturi is associated with the practical benefits of society's empirical accomplishments, appears for Roger to signify benefits to be derived only in a distinctly impalpable, distant, even metaphysical context. They are of course both right, for as this chapter has illustrated, the ambivalent connotations of such terms depend on the potential for semantic slippage, inscribed in the necessarily paradoxical perspectives of the interpreting subject. One constant, however, is the darkness and depth of nature, which in its extension to the blindness, the madness, and the sleep of the "genie," marks a space, an empty space where the perspective of the interpreter is constituted and where it has been dismantled.

Chapter III
Authority and the Strategies of the Writing Subject

The opening statement of *De l'Interprétation de la nature* has a distinctly familiar ring. For anyone versed in the queries of eighteenth-century epistemology as presented in the manifold essays and treatises on "les connaissances humaines," it is no surprise that a description of methodology for experimental philosophy—be it chemistry, biology, or physics—or for logic and grammar entails a directive to follow a procedural order intimately associated with nature, that is, a "natural order."

A short passage taken from Condillac's discussion of the process of analysis offers one among many available examples that illustrate this tendency to define the order of philosophical and scientific thought with respect to nature's order.

> Analyser n'est donc autre chose qu'observer, dans un ordre successif, les qualités d'un objet, afin de leur donner dans l'esprit l'ordre simultané dans lequel elles existent. C'est ce que la nature nous fait faire à tous.[1]

We are to understand that analysis, as a tool that dissects an object into the many attributes that constitute it, runs counter to the simultaneous order according to which this object "exists" in nature. The simultaneous order, in which the object's attributes are perceived as integral to the entity they constitute, differs conceptually from the successive order posited by analysis, in which each of the object's attributes is "abstracted" from the total impression. While the object as an integral entity loses its simultaneous form in the process of analysis,

---

1. Etienne Bonnot de Condillac, *La Logique; ou, Les premiers développements de l'Art de Penser* (Geneva: n.p., 1785), p. 19.

strangely enough this particular passage of Condillac posits the successive order as a step necessary to establish the simultaneous order.[2] In
effect, it is for the purpose ("afin de") of transforming these successive
qualities into a simultaneous order that analysis is seemingly evoked.
What is more, analysis, *like* the simultaneous order of the object existing in the mind, derives from nature as well ("c'est ce que la nature
nous fait faire à tous"). The tool of analysis seems, therefore,
implanted in nature as securely as the integral object itself. A tool of
logic performs an operation on an object seemingly at odds with the
manner in which that object is defined as existing in nature; yet,
through devious semantic and syntactical means, the analytical procedure is shown to have been generated all along by nature. Not
expressly put forward in Condillac's passage, but underlying its
ambiguous distinctions, is the relation between thought, perception
and the material object. The interrelation of these mental and material
domains is a predominant topic of consideration throughout the *philosophes'* writings. In fact, the interweaving of these three entities that
dominate epistemological structure in the eighteenth century—perception that produces a simultaneous impression of the object; analysis
that introduces a linear sequential breakdown of the object in terms of
its different attributes; the object that exists in nature—must be understood in Condillac, Diderot and the other *philosophes* with respect to
an articulation of diverse orders of language.

   The first few sentences of Diderot's treatise will engage our attention because of the way in which the question of order with relation to
observation and perception of nature's objects is specifically linked on
this particular occasion to the order of language. Most important,
Diderot's reworking of the quasi-formulaic statement distinguishing
analytic observation from perception of the object in nature to the

   2. See Dumarsais' discussion of the relation between "abstraction" and perception
in his article "Abstraction" in the *Encyclopédie, ou Dictionnaire raisonné des sciences,
des arts et des métiers*, eds. Denis Diderot et Jean D'Alembert (Berne et Lausanne:
Société typographique, 1780), vol. I. All references to the *Encyclopédie* will follow this
edition.

ends of anchoring both operations in the dynamics of nature involves, from the outset, the question of order with respect to the position of a writing subject. It is not only a question of what sort of study, of what kind of method is to be pursued in the subsequent pages. Diderot is concerned from the outset with how this order of study and observation relates to the order of his own presentation in language and, consequently, to the place of the writing subject. Why Diderot was concerned with the place of the writing subject within language has everything to do with the portrayal of his "interprète" of nature and is integral to the place of the subject in experimentation as developed in chapter II. In discussing the ramifications of Diderot's writing subject in *De l'Interprétation*, we will have occasion to broach the question of autobiographical writing in eighteenth-century literature as well as in the treatise of experimental philosophy.

Furthermore, the study of the function of language within Diderot's *Interprétation* according to the positioning of a writing subject brings into sharp focus a contrast which up to now has been viewed mainly in terms of disparate themes and according to diverse critical interpretations focusing on different aspects of Diderot's text. These first sentences of *De l'Interprétation* do not involve the dramatic opposition proclaimed by Jacques Chouillet between, on the one hand, a battle cry of the scientist and philosopher launched antagonistically against the resistance of nature and, on the other, the dream-like ecstasy of the experimental scientist as he gives himself over in a mimetic gesture to the natural forces which agitate him.[3] Rather, these initial sentences demonstrate how both personas can be operative: the writing subject like the scientist initiates an inquiry, which position of authority will

3. Venturi, Dieckmann and Chouillet have all remarked that at certain moments the experimentalist and the philosopher are identified as antagonists to nature, which on the other hand and at other places in the text is conceived as a model for imitation by the same experimental scientist and philosopher. Jacques Chouillet, *La Formation des idées esthétiques de Diderot 1745-1763* (Paris: Colin, 1973), p. 341. Franco Venturi, *op. cit.*, p. 295; Herbert Dieckmann, *Cinq Leçons sur Diderot* (Paris: Droz, 1959), pp. 41-68.

be subverted by nature's movement, strategically depicted, like the inspirational madness of genius, as originating outside and external to the narrator's own control. Here are the sentences in question:

> C'est de la nature que je vais écrire. Je laisserai les pensées se succéder sous ma plume, dans l'ordre même selon lequel les objets se sont offerts à ma réflexion; parce qu'elles n'en représenteront que mieux les mouvements et la marche de mon esprit. (*Interprétation*, p. 177)

De l'Interprétation de la nature begins by situating its object of study, nature, with relation to the writing subject. In a contrasting parallel with the initial statement of *Les Pensées philosophiques* (1746), "nature" has replaced in the work of 1754 the earlier object of stated inquiry, "Dieu": "J'écris de Dieu."[4] Along with the change in object reference there is also a deviation in the *Interprétation* from the order and verb tense of the earlier proposal. Such a transformation is revealing with respect to its model and with respect to the movement elaborated in the second, more complicated sentence of the passage in question.

The boldness of initiating a work in the first-person is mitigated in the *Interprétation* by an emphasis on the writer's object of inquiry, "nature." Precisely because of the parallel phrase in the earlier essay, pure convention can not be suspected as the reason for situating "C'est de la nature" before "je vais écrire." Emphasis on nature by its privileged position in the order of the phrase is neither simply conventional nor gratuitous. Intimated by grammatical order, the precedence of "nature" relegates the act of writing to a dependent status. In ways soon to be more amply demonstrated, it is on "nature" that the writing subject can already be seen to depend. To continue the parallel, in comparison with the immediacy evoked by "j'écris" which situates the reader at the point and moment of the narrator writing, the future

4. Denis Diderot, "Les Pensées philosophiques," *Œuvres philosophiques* (Paris: Garnier, 1964), p. 3.

immediate tense "je vais écrire" marks a distance through postponement, however short, of the act of writing.

The postponement of writing can be viewed as a function of the
dependence of the writing subject on thought, "les pensées." More
specifically, writing, in the first sentence referred to as "je vais écrire"
and carried over in the next sentence with "Je laisserai les pensées se
succéder sous ma plume," is given the status of contingency on what is
other and external to its own activity. In the same way that the syntactic position of "nature" in the first sentence suggests precedence
over the writing subject, so in the elaborate sentence which follows,
"les pensées" are shown to condition and to dominate the writing subject as, subsequently, the succession of "les pensées" will be portrayed
as contingent upon the activity of "les objets." Such a progression
leading away from the writing subject to that which is exterior to it
provides a complicated network of strategies at the syntactic as well as
the lexical level of the text.

The reader takes up a position with the writing "I" as the narrator
sketches his proposed object of study and method of procedure. This
movement corresponds on a grammatical level to the disposition of the
independent clauses. Yet, precisely by means of this apparent aim, a
project to undermine the control of the writing subject is set into place.
The central verb of the second sentence ("Je laisserai . . . se succéder")
reflects such a double movement. From one perspective, it continues
the description of the project at hand through the writing subject: the
first proposition ("C'est de la nature que je vais écrire") stating the
writer's object of study and the second elucidating the conditions or
the manner in which the narrator, the "I," will write. However, the
writing subject presents itself in an act of effacement, ceding to what is
underlined by the reflexive verb as autonomous and external to its
control: "je laisserai les pensées se succéder sous ma plume."

Several indices point to the redundance of such a message. The
complementary infinitive, the reflexive "se succéder," seems to appropriate "les pensées" which, given an anonymous status ("les"), contrast
with the possessive pronoun linked to the writer's pen, "ma plume." A

distinction is thereby secured between a passive writing subject and "pensées," active in their potential of autonomous movement. The entire sentence can be seen in effect as a series of deferrals to an externality which progressively informs the writing subject as passive first to "pensées" as then "pensées" cede to "objets." It is in the subordinate clause "dans l'ordre même selon lequel les objets se sont offerts" that the process of writing seems to be grounded. In one respect, each clause contains the same pattern of contrast between the subject and that which is external to it and autonomous. Such a pattern is easily discernible by the disposition of clauses without their interconnections:

> —Les pensées se succéder sous ma plume . . .
> —les objets se sont offerts à ma reflexion . . .
> —les mouvements et la marche de mon esprit.

In each of the phrases "thoughts," "objects" and "movements" are juxtaposed with relation to a noun in all three cases modified by the possessive pronoun "my." The similarity of construction is quite striking, especially in the first two phrases where there is an exact duplication of grammatical order: definite article, noun, reflexive verb, preposition, possessive adjective and noun.

The above stated order ascribes to "pensées" the same status as "objets" through repeated delineation of and contrast with the explicitly subjective elements, "ma plume," "ma réflexion," and "mon esprit" which are portrayed as passive. In other words, the strategy at work in these phrases presents the narrator's intentions to direct his writing towards a certain project while undermining an autonomous, active writing subject and, consequently, defining writing as originating elsewhere. This can be seen clearly by the way in which the successive phrases mentioned above are strung out linearly in syntactic relation to each other. Not only is there an increase in the active role of "objets" which "se sont offerts" in comparison with "se succéder" which passively modifies "les pensées," but the latter become dependent on "objets" in both a temporal as well as a grammatical causality.

The mechanism of deferral employed in this long sentence springs grammatically from the manner in which, through its reading, a phrase achieves self-containment just at the point or moment it is to be subsumed and appropriated by what follows: "Je laisserai les pensées se succéder sous ma plume," is prolonged, reopened, after the comma emphasizing the phrase's integrity, by a proposition which gives, in retrospect, another basis to "pensées." The abstract quality of "thoughts" is exchanged for "objects" which, retroactively, validate "thoughts" by giving them a new basis or grounding. Authentification of "thoughts" depends therefore not upon thought itself but on the extent to which thought is other than itself—to the extent to which "pensées" are "objets."

There is also, as stated above, a temporal causality linked to the precedence or anteriority of "objets." Whereas all verbs speaking to the activity of the writing or representing subject are rendered in a form of the future tense ("je vais écrire," "je laisserai se succéder," "elles représenteront"), the dependent clause concerning the appearance of "objets" has already taken place in the past. Following this chronology, the sentence can be read backwards, beginning with "objets" and, given their exteriority to subject, their assumed partaking of the external world; their impact on reflection produces thoughts flowing under the pen, which constitutes the impetus for "je vais écrire." Such a chronological reading would invert the grammatical order by situating "objets" as the original controlling force guiding the sentence as well as the mental operation. The independent and dependent clauses of the sentence would consequently be reversed, relegating the verbs of the writing subject to dependent status whereas the independent clauses would feature the active agent—intimated, alluded to, in the actual sentence order: "objets," "nature."

The final clause adjoined to the preceding series in the actual sentence refers back to "pensées" with the pronoun "elles." The reversal hypothesized in a chronological reading of the initial sentence order in effect takes place with the second independent clause. Consonant with the previous mention of the grammatical mechanism of deferral, the sentence is extended anew, after a semi-colon, with the added conjunction "parce que." However, disrupting the order of antecedents and the movement from the writing subject to that which is progressively more external to it, "objets" are not to be redefined; rather, it is "pensées" which, having been grounded on the order of "objets," can now be reinstated in a position of prime importance.

A kind of conflation has been effected between the entities "pensées" and "objets." Because of its proximity with "objets" as well as with the forceful connective "parce que," "elles" seems to relate to the preceding clause and to "objets" as an antecedent instead of to "pensées"; therefore "elles" appears to relate to the primary and fundamental order imposed by the anteriority of "objets." Now, however, those thoughts, having been both grammatically and semantically alienated from the control of a writing subject and appropriated by "objets," acquire an active power of representation ("parce qu'elles n'en représenteront que mieux les mouvements et la marche de mon esprit"). If "pensées" have been appropriated by the assumed external world of "objets," they now function tautologically to "represent" the movement of the mind. On one level, this can be understood as the final step in the extroversion of the writing subject. From the contrast between a passive writing subject and the final statement of the mind's "mouvements" and "marche" there has been a conversion through which the subject has taken on the attributes of its own exteriority.

Through a metonymy of substitution, "les mouvements et la marche" partake of the order in which objects offered themselves and thoughts succeeded themselves. In effect, the movement here traced parallels the previous subordination of "pensées" to "objets." "Objets" is to "pensées" in the first part of the sentence as "pensées" is to "esprit" in the last clause. Once "objectified," "pensées," coming so to speak from outside the mind and adhering to the order of things, inform "esprit" with an alterity in relation to the writing or narrating subject. The contradictions attendant on such strategy become immediately apparent. "Les pensées" in their initial separation from the writing subject are made to represent "objets"; they are then enlisted to represent "l'esprit." Through a mechanism of metonymy, "pensées" then becomes a term which functions in opposite, contrasting modes.

No longer deriving their origin in the mind, "pensées" are free to return to the mind as different from it. Yet, its initial status having been lost or supplemented, there is an ensuing loss of distinction between "pensées" and "objets," between "pensées" and "esprit," between "objets" and "esprit." The introduction of "esprit" in the last clause has in a way already been divested of its subjective properties. There exists an evident gap or separation from the writing subject situated at the beginning of the sentence. In effect, "pensées" are no longer connected to writing. They now "represent" the movement of the mind.

With the substitution of "représenter" for writing lies the final deferral to what derives outside and external to the writing subject. The structure of the last proposition reverses the order to be found in the first clauses. Whereas the writing subject is also the subject of the independent verb in the main clause, leaving the dependent clauses to usurp the active role of the subject, "pensées" now actively represent the subject "esprit"—in the future. "Représenter" by the very nature of its lexical value alludes to a doubling, a re-presenting of the object of study, whereas the theme of writing is relegated to words and to a subject responsible for them. The personal agent of this process has been eliminated, while representation alludes to a transparency of object and mind.

The status of the above sentences with regard to the text of the *Interprétation* as a whole merits special attention. By the apparent intent of the writing subject posited at the beginning of the work to describe the nature of the text to follow, it would appear that we are dealing with a meta-statement, with a statement situated outside of, before or after, the text as a whole. The import of these sentences of Diderot is to instate "nature," "objets" over the writing subject as originator and organizer of the text. Yet, by their position and formal syntax, these phrases claim to be a personal invocation, a sui-referential meta-statement. A cursory look at the ways in which a sui-referential meta-statement assumes significance in narrative structures within different genres will locate it with respect to traditional usage as well as demonstrate its extremely paradoxical status in the *Interprétation*. Such a discussion also reveals a poetics specific to certain aspects of scientific, historical, and fictional narratives.

The question of a sui-referential meta-statement is posed by Roland Barthes with specific attention to "le discours de l'histoire."[5] And while historical discourse is likened by Barthes to fictional discourse, the narrative structure of Diderot's treatise bears resemblance in certain respects to both historical and fictional narrative. Barthes attempts to demystify "objective history" through his study of historical narrative within the categories of a linguistic theory of discourse.[6] In effect, the author has elaborated Benveniste's distinction between "discours" and "récit historique" to new ends. Barthes' article intimates a conflation of the two poles introduced by the linguist.[7]

5. Roland Barthes, "Discours de l'histoire," *Information sur les sciences sociales* IV (August 1967), 65-75, repr. in *Le Bruissement de la langue, Essais Critiques IV* (Paris: Seuil, 1984), pp. 153-66.

6. Roland Barthes, "Introduction à l'analyse structurale des récits," *Communications* 8 (1966), repr. in *L'Analyse structurale du récit* (Paris: Seuil, 1981), pp. 7-33. In this slightly earlier article, Barthes proposes general linguistics as a model for discourse analysis. The development of such rules of discourse in function of their literary application would, according to Barthes: "constitute même l'une des premières tâches de la sémiologie" ("Discours de l'histoire," p. 65): "Quoi que constituant un objet autonome, c'est à partir de la linguistique que le discours doit être étudié; s'il faut donner une hypothèse de travail à une analyse dont la tâche est immense et les matériaux infinis, le plus raisonnable est de postuler un rapport homologique entre la phrase et le discours, dans la mesure où une même organisation formelle règle vraisemblablement tous les systèmes sémiotiques, quelles qu'en soient les substances et les dimensions: le discours serait une grande 'phrase' (dont les unités ne sauraient être nécessairement des phrases), tout comme la phrase, moyennant certaines spécifications, est un petit 'discours' " (*Communications*, p. 3).

7. Emile Benveniste, "Les Relations de temps dans le verbe français," *Problèmes de linguistique générale* (Paris: Gallimard, 1966), I, 237-50. A reference to Benveniste at this point is in keeping with the context Barthes himself invokes. To situate Barthes' use of the title "Discours de l'histoire," it is necessary to introduce certain distinctions made by Benveniste. For the linguist, "il faut entendre discours dans sa plus large

Benveniste's opposition between "discours" and historical narrative or "récit" is transformed in both the title and content of Barthes' article, becoming the "discours de l'histoire." If Benveniste sees in historical writing an aim to represent itself as recounting the "real" through an insistence on events defined as exterior to the present utterance, Barthes addresses himself to the narrative complements of this language as strategies akin to those at work in fiction.

A major claim of historical narrative, in Barthes' words, is to "exprimer le réel." This bears direct comparison with Diderot's emphasis in the *Interprétation*. In both contexts, the definition of the "real" depends on its separation from all marks of the first-person and the present utterance. As Diderot states elsewhere in the text:

> Tant que les choses ne sont que dans *notre* entendement ce sont *nos* opinions; ce sont des notions qui peuvent être vraies ou fausses, accordées ou contredites. Elles ne prennent de la consistence qu'en se liant aux *êtres extérieurs*. (*Interprétation*, p. 184, my emphasis)

The process of exteriorization analyzed in the first sentences of Diderot's text parallels the way of knowing for the experimental scien-

---

extension: toute énonciation supposant un locuteur et un auditeur, et chez le premier l'intention d'influencer l'autre en quelque manière" (Benveniste, pp. 241-42). Historical narrative contrasts with "discours" in that: "Il faut et il suffit que l'auteur reste fidèle à son propos d'historien et qu'il proscrive tout ce qui est étranger au récit des événements (discours, réflexions, comparaisons): A vrai dire, il n'y a même plus alors de narrateur. Les événements sont posés comme ils se sont produits à mesure qu'ils apparaissent à l'horizon de l'histoire. Personne ne parle ici; les événements semblent se raconter eux-mêmes. Le temps fondamental est l'aoriste, qui est le temps de l'événement hors de la personne d'un narrateur" (Benveniste, p. 241).

Discourse corresponds on the level of language to those pronouns (*je-tu*), adverbs (*ici-maintenant, là-alors*) and verb tenses (all except the aoriste or passé simple), which relate to the event in the past and to that which is exterior to the present enunciation: "Car dès qu'on ne vise plus, par l'expression même, cette relation de l'indicateur à l'instance unique qui le manifeste, la langue recourt à une série de termes distincts qui correspondent un à aux premiers et qui se réfèrent, non plus à l'instance de discours, mais aux objets 'réels', aux temps et lieux historiques" (Benveniste, I, 254).

tist: knowledge must be transparent to its referent, nature. Barthes' definition of historical discourse emphasizes this discipline's claim to the "real." Such writing denies itself except as "la copie pure et simple d'une autre existence, située dans un champ extrastructural, 'le réel' " (Barthes, p. 73).

Why and in what manner then does the author of historical and of scientific discourse call attention to his own writing, his own organization of events and of nature within a language which endeavors to be neutral and "objective"? Sui-reference of the writing subject takes place, according to Barthes, in the context of two basic categories. The second corresponds explicitly to the situation of Diderot's meta-statement and includes: "tous les signes par lesquels l'énonçant organise son propre discours, le reprend, le modifie en cours de route, en un mot y dispose des repères explicites" (Barthes, p. 67). The sub-category of the inaugurations of historical discourse include prospectives on the works such as the preface as well as what Barthes terms "l'ouverture performative":

> Le discours de l'histoire connaît en général deux formes d'inauguration; tout d'abord ce que l'on pourrait appeler l'ouverture performative, car la parole y est véritablement un acte solennel de fondation; le modèle en est poétique, c'est le "je chante" des poètes. (Barthes, p. 67)

Barthes disagrees with the traditional explanation of the presence of the narrator within his own text in such an instance as solemnly demonstrating the need for subjective expression. Such a factor "a moins pour but de donner à l'historien une possibilité d'exprimer sa subjectivité comme on le dit communément, que de compliquer le temps chronique de l'histoire en l'affrontant à un autre temps, qui est celui du discours lui-même" (Barthes, p. 67).

In Diderot's opening statement, there is an interesting opposition to Barthes' definition of the personal and poetic invocation as explicit admission of a time other than the linear time of past events. The mytho-poetic necessity, which incites the narrator to predict or to identify himself with the all-knowing organization of time, finds a contrast in the sentences of the *Interprétation* analyzed above. For precisely the position of fore-knowledge and organization is explicitly renounced in favor of a time as well as in favor of an order intrinsic to the main body of the text. Reference to the present utterance is avoided through the consistent use of the future tense in all first-person verbs. The future reference corresponds to a deferral of the time of writing to the time and order of "objets"—to be the time of the text itself. The precedence or anteriority of "objets" once posited as the origin of writing, the subject will transcribe the dictation of the referent.

In the renunciation of the privileged perspective in the above variation of "je chante" as organizing principle of the text, the "je," the writing subject, is evoked for precisely the opposite reason. The writing subject appears as authenticated not by implied reference to the extra-textual muses of myth; rather, the authority of the narrative voice is established in as much as the text to follow partakes of the external world and can be consistently guaranteed itself to precede the writing "I."

This particular situation evidenced in Diderot's text finds a parallel in the structure of certain eighteenth-century novels. In memoir fiction such as *La Vie de Marianne* the narrator relates in the first-person the events of her life. "Je conte ma vie," the opening statement of the novel, is studied by Jean Rousset as an example of a narrative of convergence:

> On retiendra donc un double effet de convergence, la coïncidence du narrateur et du personnage raconté, la simultanéité de la rédaction et d'une part au moins de l'action racontée dans la mesure où il est fait usage du présent.[8]

But the past is represented, for the most part, not in terms of the narrator's reaction through her present consciousness to events and situa-

---

8. Jean Rousset, *Narcisse Romancier: Essai sur la première personne dans le roman* (Paris: Corti, 1973), p. 17.

tions which would disrupt and fragment the initial order. Rather, it is in chronological order, proceeding from the earliest events through her life up to the present that Marianne tells her story. Rousset terms this double persona an "unité narcissique," insisting that "l'instance narrative 'Je conte' et l'objet narré, 'mon histoire' constituent une unité, marquée par le pronom et le possessif de première personne" (Rousset, p. 16). Yet, though they refer to the same person, the possessive pronoun in the objective case stresses the duality in which " 'je conte' est un présent, 'mon histoire', 'ma vie' sont du passé par rapport à ce moment où l'on parle" (Rousset, p. 17).

A disjunction of the narrating "je" with the events recounted endows the character with a certain "objective" status by immersing the individual entity within a chronology of historical verisimilitude. The objects, the people which make up Marianne's life and experiences take to some degree precedence over the product of her present consciousness that can not truly reorder nor redefine her life from a new perspective. On the other hand, the identity or similarity of the enunciating "je" with the person involved in those past events emphasizes an attempt to appropriate such objective reality to the writing subject, to corroborate the individual experience with its historical counterpart.

The relation of the narrating "je" in the first phrases of Diderot's *Interprétation* to "pensées," to "objets" is parallel to the narrative "je" as it functions in *La Vie de Marianne*. To the extent "pensées" in Diderot's text are qualified as external to purely subjective thought, as succeeding in chronological order like "objets," and simultaneously, as intrinsic to the writing "je," these "thoughts" occupy the same position as the succeeding events of "ma vie" with relation to Marianne's "je conte." The parallel function of these writing narratives serves to underline a strategy which is also a poetics through which to attain objective status for the narrative voice by appropriating, after the fact, the concrete givens of the "what really happened."

Thus, it may be, as Barthes maintains, that the suppression of the sui-referential writing subject can be traced to the notion of "objectivity" in genres such as the *romanesque* as well as in historical and scientific-philosophical narratives. However, the very use of "je" as writing or narrating subject might be studied in terms of its explicit representation as other than the organizing principle of the text. As indicated by my example, the use of the first-person writing, narrating subject can indicate a strategy by which a historical fact, a physical or material entity or event is evoked as external to it and by this means is lent the authority to formulate, to articulate, the narrating subject. In this instance, the role of "je" is circumscribed by its defined contingence on what is portrayed as other than and exterior to itself while it is, of course, through this very distinction from "je" that within writing an external or material domain can be represented. The authority of the writing, narrating subject is ostensibly dismantled while on the rhetorical level, it continues to figure in a dominating capacity.

The question of an objective illusion then is to be discerned not only where there is elimination of all reference to a narrating subject, or for that matter an exclusive use of the third-person pronoun ("la personne objective") which Barthes terms a "significant absence." The first-person sui-referential form of discourse can function according to a certain poetics as absence, as expicitly other than the organizing principle of the text: "Je est un autre," or to the extent that such a formula is recognized as a strategy of narration, " 'Je' est un autre."

The strategic use of "je" in the opening phrases of the *Interprétation* marks a situation crucial to the thematic as well as to the grammatical level of the text. The innovation effected in Diderot's use of the sui-referential invocation formula resides in the locating of a source external, as with the muses, to the writing subject but internal to the text itself. To the extent that "je" is syntactically constituted by its relation to "objet," text becomes like nature, replacing the narrator's word with the physical world. What precedes the writing subject is not as in the traditional "je chante" a validation of the poet or historian's words as informed by the presence of another language, the divine language of myth; rather, the object "represented" can validate language in as much as writing is homogenous with its object, which is to say, in as much as language can be different from itself, transparent to the world it imitates, and finally, in as much as writing is continuously postponed to an indefinite future.

The textual strategy elaborated by such a poetics can be historically situated as Barthes demonstrates in his article, "Science versus Literature."[9] Language has been progressively considered as "subordinate to the matter of science (its workings, hypotheses, results) which, so it is said, exists outside of language and precedes it." Barthes alludes to a decline in the status of language from the sixteenth century to contemporary times:

> It is not a coincidence that, from the sixteenth century onwards, the corporate blossoming of empiricism, rationalism and an evidential religion (with the Reformation), that is, of the scientific spirit in the widest sense of the term, should have been accompanied by a regression in the autonomy of language, henceforth relegated to the rank of instrument or "fine style," whereas in the Middle Ages human culture had shared out the secrets of speech and nature almost equally, under the headings of the Seven Liberal Arts. (Barthes, p. 411)

Diderot attempts to effect a merging of discourse with nature, as seen in the opening statement, by a strategic positioning of writing subject with regard to "objets" which dominate and which, as Barthes says in a more general but perfectly applicable comment:

> exist outside of language and [precede] it. On the one hand, the *first*, there is the content of the scientific message which is everything; on the other hand and *next*, the verbal form responsible for expressing that content, which is nothing. (Barthes, p. 411, Barthes' emphasis)

9. Roland Barthes, "Sciences Versus Literature," *Introduction to Structuralism*, ed. Michael Lane (New York: Harper, 1970), pp. 410-16. Article reprinted from *Times Literary Supplement* (September 28, 1967); also repr. as "De la science à la litterature," dans *Le Bruissement de la langue, op. cit.*, pp. 13-20.

Of course, language must be well-wrought in order to present itself as untainted by its own premises. Diderot's position occupies a mid-point in such a chronology of language's rhetoric on its own function. In the narrative voice of the first-person, the reader can still view the series of procedures which, in later scientific treatises as well as in the novel, are to cede to other rhetorical practices in the voice of the third-person, the "non-personne" as Benveniste terms it, and in the "positive content" of empiricism.

On the thematic level of the *Interprétation,* therefore, an important parallel presents itself between the writing subject as portrayed in the opening phrases of this work and the ideal scientist and philosopher-subject as he pursues and conjectures nature's secrets. The gauge of authentic scientific project and results will be the extent to which the subject, the observing experimenting scientist, is rendered passive by that which is forever external to his individual capabilities of organiz-ing and of pre-ordering knowledge. At the same time, it is from the perspective of the scientist and philosopher that the possibility of knowing nature exists. *De l'Interprétation de la nature* is specifically dedicated and directed to the young natural philosopher whose tech-niques and goals Diderot has ostensibly set out to influence.[10] If Diderot conducts his description and inquiry into "experimental physics" according to the scientist who is to manipulate, to experiment with, nature, it is precisely upon the conversion of scientist as subject to scientist as receiver of nature that such an orientation depends.

Chapters II and III have demonstrated that the interpreter and the narrator constitute the orienting and the controlling element of a project as well as of a discourse which must always either defer to the future or, chiasmatically, must come after in the wake of a force other than and external to its own. In the complex syntax, grammar and semantics of the *Interprétation*'s opening sentences, the position of the writing subject produces and is a function of the difference between

10. The dedication is entitled: "Aux Jeunes Gens qui se Disposent à l'Etude de la Philosophie Naturelle" (Editions Garnier), p. 175.

writing and representation. How that difference comes to be established in the text stems from a narrative first-person perspective introduced only to be subverted in the subsequent interrelation of the dependent clauses. Such a discrepancy between writing and representation, between discourse and image, plays an integral role throughout *De l'Interprétation de la nature*; this poetics coincides with the opposition thematically elaborated, as we will see in chapter IV, between metaphysics and experimental, natural science, and between discourse and image.

Chapter IV
Representation and the Poetics of Nature in the *Interprétation*

La philosophie, comme théorie de la métaphore, aura d'abord été une métaphore de la théorie. Cette circulation n'a pas exclu, a permis et provoqué au contraire la transformation de la présence en présence a soi, en proximité ou propriété de la subjectivité à elle-même. C'est l'histoire du sens "propre" dont il faudrait suivre le détour et le retour. (Derrida, *Marges*, p. 309)

It is with regard to a particular perspective that the initial tenets of *De l'Interprétation de la nature* are introduced. Fragments II-IV present the case for what Diderot discerns as a "moment d'une grande révolution dans les sciences" (fr. IV). Such a turning point is marked by a validation of the "physical,"[1] as opposed to the mathematical sciences, through a contrast drawn between the realm of the abstract and the concrete domain of "notre terre":

Une des vérités qui aient été annoncées de nos jours avec le plus de courage et de force, qu'un bon physicien ne perdra point de vue et qui aura certainement les suites les plus avantageuses; c'est que la région des mathématiques est un monde intellectuel, où ce que l'on prend pour des vérités rigoureuses perd absolument cet avantage quand on l'apporte sur notre terre. (*Interprétation*, fr. II, p. 178)

The long series of phrases evoking but deferring the announcement of a new truth finally reaches its objective with an inverse and deflated

---

1. In view of the contrast specifically drawn between the realm of the concrete and that of the abstract, I will retain Diderot's term "sciences physiques" in keeping with the intended opposition to "sciences métaphysiques." The term "physique expérimentale" corresponds today to physics, chemistry, physiology and experimental biology. See Herbert Dieckmann, *Cinq leçons sur Diderot*, p. 53.

statement. The reader awaits an explanation of the initial clause ("une des vérités qui aient été annoncées de nos jours") throughout the duration of the sentence, which terminates with a focus on what is antagonistic to the new truth. As opposed to calling up the protagonist, "physique expérimentale," the sentence, like the science of mathematics, comes to completion on the absence of positive results. The long trip down from the abstract skies of mathematics to the region of "notre terre" is parodied in the laborious syntax of a sentence which leads to a loss ("où ce que l'on prend pour des vérités rigoureuses *perd* absolument cet avantage") with respect to the perspective which is termed "notre." Upon this negatively stated truth and criterion the grammatical sentence depends. From this contrasting perspective, the science of mathematics has been represented.

The "transcendent" region of mathematics (*Interprétation*, p. 179) has been juxtaposed along a vertical axis to the "grounding" metaphor of "notre terre" which replaces the former discipline with a concreteness guaranteed by a perspective that leaves the elaboration of abstract truths to the formal intellectual "jeux" or conventions of mathematics.[2] Chapter II has already demonstrated the opposition of abstract concepts with the earthly, indeed subterranean, regions of the experimenter's fruitful groping. The "earth" then continues to operate as a dominant metaphor in the *Interprétation*. And as we saw in chapters II and III, its use is consistently linked to the perspective of the experimenter as well as to that of the narrator. In effect, the entity of the material world begins to acquire a certain textual density through a strategic positioning of the subject pronouns, the possessive adjectives and their coordinates that constitute first-person discourse.

---

2. Fragment III elaborates a comparison between the "conventions" of "jeu" and those of mathematics along lines of an opposition drawn between "chose" and a series of rules established without regard to any natural process or object: "Je ne sais s'il y a quelque rapport entre l'esprit de jeu et le génie mathématicien; mais il y en a beaucoup entre un jeu et les mathématiques. . . . Il n'y a point de questions de mathématiques à qui la même définition ne puisse convenir, et la *chose* du mathématicien n'a pas plus d'existence dans la nature que celle du joueur. C'est de part et d'autre, une affaire de convention." (*Interprétation*, fr. III, p. 179, Diderot's emphasis).

As we saw earlier, the place of the first-person is neither stable, nor is it always situated as in the above example of "notre terre" to denote a contrast to metaphysical abstractions. The domain of "notre" fragments into a division where the signs "notre," "nos," "je" and their appropriate verbs are also to be found on the opposite side of concrete knowledge and results:

> Tant que les choses ne sont que dans *notre* entendement ce sont *nos* opinions; ce sont des notions, qui peuvent être vraies ou fausses, accordées ou contredites. Elles ne prennent de la consistence qu'en se liant aux êtres *extérieurs*. (*Interprétation*, fr. VII, p. 184, my emphasis)

The criteria of validity for scientific research are to be located within our own lives and functions as biological, physiological entities within an organic material world where, as opposed to the metaphysical concept, "les corps" will not be "dépouillés de leurs qualités individuelles" (*Interprétation*, fr. II, p. 179). The measure of results in such a science, however, is represented by the extent to which the perspective of the first-person, in this instance, "nous," is surpassed by what can be defined as external to it. Strikingly similar to Buffon's statement that "les vérités ne dépendent pas de nous,"[3] Diderot's formula demonstrates an orientation toward the world of matter and of the senses which Locke and Condillac, to name two of his predecessors, had done so much to advance.

A growing emphasis on the natural sciences in the eighteenth century appears to coincide with a particular interest in epistemological distinctions between sense perception and abstract thought. An emphasis, however, on the material world as perceived through the senses and as distinct from abstract thought, presented new problems. How to assure an adequation of sense perception with the physical object world without implying individual distortion and, consequently, without blurring the distinctions between the properties of percep-

---

3. See my chapter II, p. 50.

tion and those of abstract, even arbitrary, operations of the mind? Integral to the new priority of natural science is an attempt to surpass the isolated "cogito" of the cartesian system, to reach a material realm not ordered in advance by the preconceived categories of metaphysics centered on an individual system and consciousness.[4] One of the ways this new ordering takes place within the text is through the modes of representation where an opposition can be drawn along the horizontal axis of the inside/outside of the experimenting subject. This chapter will concentrate specifically on the complex textual dynamics that articulate an interiority/exteriority of the experimenting subject, and will follow the concurrent development of a pertinent distinction in Diderot's *Interprétation* between descriptive and discursive writing, between image and text.

The relocation and redefinition of the perspective of the subject as experimental scientist and as writing subject has been studied in chapters II and III with emphasis on demonstrating how the intuitive experimental genius and writing subject originate in and/or are dependent on external phenomena. This chapter will continue to trace this

---

4. Locke begins his treatise with the now famous denial of both innate principles and innate ideas. John Locke, *An Essay Concerning Human Understanding*, ed. A. C. Fraser (New York: Dover, 1959), Bk. I, ch. I, II, pp. 38-118. For Condillac, see Etienne Bonnot de Condillac, *Essai sur l'Origine des Connaissances Humaines*, précédé de "l'Archéologie du frivole," par Jacques Derrida, édité par Charles Porset (Paris: Galilée, 1973). Any reference to this work of Condillac will be quoted from the above edition in the text of my chapters IV and V. See especially in the *Essai*, 1ière partie, "Des Matériaux de nos connaissances et particulièrement des opérations de l'âme," ch. I, II. See also Condillac, *Traité sur les sensations* in *Œuvres complètes*, ed. Georges le Roy, Corpus Général des philosophes français (Paris: P.U.F., 1947). Apart from the *Essai*, citation of all other works of Condillac will refer to the above edition. Aram Vartanian states the view of these sensualists quite succinctly: "The theory of Locke and Condillac, which in tracing all ideas fundamentally to sensory experience of the outside world, had provided the epistemological underpinnings of the experimentalist-inductive method," *Diderot and Descartes* (Princeton University Press, 1953), p. 182. In the context of this remark it is interesting to note that the original title of Condillac's *Essai* in 1746 had been: "Essai sur l'Origine des connaissances humaines où l'on réduit à un *seul principe* tout ce qui concerne l'entendement humain" (my emphasis).

perspective and will entail an expansion of the gesture previously iden-tified. The need to posit the perspective of the scientist as well as nar-rator with regard to an alterity, to a material or concrete "real" from which the subject is then reinformed and assimilated into its "other," involves a complicated series of textual maneuvers. Stated at its most basic level, two movements can be discerned in the text: a presentation of subject in a manner so as to introduce and to separate off what is portrayed as existing beyond it; from this distinction evolves the opposite movement which progressively informs the subject anew, at this point, with those attributes of its own exteriority.

Modern linguistic theory sheds light on this situation in its elabora-tion of the use of pronouns whose schema can be seen to function in fragment VII of the *Interprétation*. Repeated emphasis there on the possessive pronoun and adjective "nous," "nos," creates the poles of its complementary opposite, "êtres extérieurs." According to Benveniste, there is no way to refer to an "il," or by extension, to an exteriority, except from the position of subject or interiority:

> Il faut garder à l'esprit que la "3ième personne" est la forme du para-digme verbal (ou pronominal) qui ne renvoie *pas* à une personne, parce qu'elle se réfère à un objet placé hors de l'allocution. Mais elle n'existe et ne se caractérise que par opposition à la personne *je* du locuteur qui, l'énonçant, la situe comme "non-personne." C'est là son statut. La forme "il" . . . tire sa valeur de ce qu'elle fait nécessairement partie d'un discours énoncé par "je." (Benveniste's emphasis)[5]

It is not possible to refer to what is explicitly external to the subject in discourse without appropriating language through "je," or in this case, "nous." The textual strategy to be studied in the *Interprétation* involves a movement of separation of the subject from object as well as certain mechanisms employed to overcome the seeming impossibil-ity of endowing the material world as represented in the text (through

5. Emile Benveniste, *op. cit.*, I, 265.

distinction from and difference with the subject) with the power to give form to the subject. As stated above in the words of Benveniste: "La forme 'il' . . . tire sa valeur de ce qu'elle fait nécessairement partie d'un discours énoncé par 'je.' " How is it possible for Diderot's text to shift perspective such that alterity to the enunciator of discourse, to the interpreter of nature, can precede, can evoke, can inform "je"? In other words, how to enact within a verbal context, the priority of nature's material domain, of nature's object?

We have seen that the portrayal of the "true" observer/interpreter of nature in the *Interprétation* always entails a necessary expropriation of certain qualities inherent in the reasoned and consistent awareness of the rational scientist. It is also important to examine more specifically the other side of this expropriation of the subject. In effect, an assimilation of subject into its alterity takes place through a transference, or in rhetorical terms, by means of metonymy. Through the preservation of an additional and alien element in the subject's activity (the subject unlike itself), a metonymic chain is initiated. As it turns out, that additional element in the subject's activity partakes of the material, object world as a part participates in the whole.

A good illustration of this metonymic chain which serves to separate and to distinguish subject from object as well as to render the experimenting, writing subject a function of object is Diderot's elaboration of "les lois de l'investigation de la vérité" (fr. IX, p. 185). This fragment is traditionally cited as evidence of the author's profound understanding of and contribution to the new emerging scientific methodology: "Tout se réduit à revenir des sens à la réflexion, et de la réflexion aux sens: rentrer en soi et en sortir sans cesse" (*Interprétation,* fr. IX, p. 185).[6] Experimental science involves a process of investigation inclusive of observation gleaned in the field as well as of reflection

---

6. Jacques Roger, *op. cit.,* p. 604. Jacques Chouillet, *La Formation des idées esthétiques* (Paris: Colin, 1973), p. 334. Roger employs this fragment, as Chouillet points out, to show a substitution "aux démarches de la philosophie rationnelle, le vrai mouvement de la pensée scientifique."

on those experimental data. If the initial opposition senses/reflection corresponds indeed to the dual mental and physiological disposition of the experimenter, this fragment also bears witness to a parallel but different opposition, formulated in terms of self/other which, while appearing to formulate a four-term analogy, actually displaces the initial duality.

On the one hand, the senses are defined by a relation of difference through a spatial metaphor that distances them from reflection ("revenir des sens à la réflexion") and, vice versa, "réflexion" is defined through its differential relation to "sens." Senses and reflection are seen to fulfill complementary functions of the feeling, observing, thinking individual. This supposedly analogous or parallel elucidation of the opposition senses/reflection reveals in fact a new polarity: self/other. The new contrast outlines a sharper distinction than that evidenced between senses and reflection. But to the extent the second polarity establishes a parallel clarification of the first, as the colon indicates, the status of the first opposition changes. "Senses" must now, in retrospect, be viewed not in terms of the subject who perceives the material world by means of the agents of sight, taste, touch, etc.; rather, on the model of the opposition self/other, the senses have become a metonymy for the material world itself. To the extent the senses are qualified by a movement away ("en sortir") from "soi" and distinct from the process which qualifies "réflexion" as a return to "soi" ("rentrer en soi"), the senses themselves have already distinctly been displaced to a domain marginal to the circumscribed integral subject. The seeing, feeling, tasting, hearing of the experimentalist begin to be exchanged for what is now suggested to be external, material or real causes. The senses, therefore, are to a certain extent not always to be defined as what inheres in the individual but can be informed (as will be seen more clearly in the following fragment) as that which inheres in the properties of things.

The progressive distancing of the object world from "soi" substantiates the realm of external entities. This is evidenced in the further distinction of senses/reflection according to the dichotomy self/other, "soi"/outside "soi." Yet, the ambivalence of the term "senses" as it functions in the text also produces the opposite movement. In as much an attribute of the human constitution, senses are also defined in this fragment as inherent in the subject. It is no coincidence that the movement defined in both clauses begins at the point of returning to its opposite, to self. "Revenir des sens à la réflexion" and "rentrer en soi" emphasize the circularity of a continuous movement; nevertheless, the description of such circularity is initiated at the moment of returning to reflection, which when further elaborated signifies a return to "soi."

As the progression augments to distinguish and separate "senses" from "reflection," and then, outside "soi" from "soi," so augments also the rapidity with which "self" is informed by its other, becomes its other. A rapid exchange insists on the reciprocity of a movement which covers the poles of the very antinomy evoked. "Soi"/outside "soi" is a more radical opposition than "senses"/"reflection"; however, the movement from one to the other is simultaneous with the closing of the gap: "rentrer en soi et en sortir sans cesse."

> C'est le travail de l'abeille. On a battu bien du terrain en vain, si on ne rentre pas dans la ruche chargée de cire. On a fait bien des amas de cire inutile, si on ne sait pas en former des rayons. (*Interprétation*, fr. IX, p. 185)[7]

Use of the bee image continues the double movement of separation and unity described in the first part of this fragment. On the one hand, it provides a parallel distinction between two poles; on the other, it continues the work of assimilation through metonymy. If the senses are intimated by the self/other polarity to be situated outside "soi" and therefore to partake of the external world, the addition of the bee

---

7. The bee image in the service of experimental philosophy comes from Bacon, "Novum Organum," *Opera Omnia, op. cit.*, I, IXCV, p. 310. See Dieckmann's mention of this image in "The Influence of Francis Bacon on Diderot's *Interprétation*," p. 311.

image furthers such assimilation. For the work of the true physicist on analogy with the work of the animals partakes of a process as it is elaborated and accomplished in nature. As in the polarity self/other, two movements are defined in the different objectives of "ruche" and "rayon"; and the potential similarity of the two poles is effected by the use of two terms which resemble each other alliteratively as well as semantically.[8] Yet, the analogy with the first part of the fragment is distinctly not perfect as the two poles remain both exterior to the bee even if "rentrer dans la ruche" is a close approximation of "rentrer en soi." In effect, the image of the bee serves to substitute a polarity less ambiguous than the distinctions made earlier in the text. But the importance of the bee image lies not with an exact or less than perfect duplication of the aforementioned antimonies. Its importance resides in the shift to a new level of representation that coincides with one element in the polarity, the exteriority of nature itself.

A further assimilation is effected of the work of the "physicien" to the natural world through the comparison with the work of the bee. This image serves to separate, or rather, to separate further the polarities sense/reflection, outside/inside "soi." In effect, the first sentence of the next fragment (fr. X, p. 185) brings the series of differentiations to its ultimate stage in the opposition "nature"/"soi": "Mais il est plus court de se consulter soi que la nature." The above image of the bees has served to elaborate on the procedure of the observing subject as analogous to a natural process. In other words, the seemingly innocent comparison is at the same time a model for where and how the scientist should elaborate his concepts, that is to say, according to an exteriority within nature itself. And this exteriority is represented within Diderot's text at the level of image which corresponds,

---

8. According to *Robert*, "ruche" refers to the "abri aménagé pour y recevoir un essaim d'abeilles," whereas "rayon" refers to "chaque gâteau de cire formé par certains insectes et dont les alvéoles ou cellules sont remplies de miel." Mentioned, however, as "usage vieux," "ruche" can also indicate "chacun des alvéoles du gâteau de cire contenant le miel."

therefore, to one aspect of the polarity, "outside soi." This pictorial representation of nature relates to the initial, more abstract formulation of the first part of the fragment as the entity "senses" was related to "soi." The substitution of a textual image for the more discursive and conceptual prose of the initial formulation illustrates therefore a distinct parallel between the poetics and the methodology of science.[9]

Another textual comparison that elicits a pictorial representation integral to the particular orientation of the scientific endeavor described can be seen in the preceding fragment VIII:

> On peut comparer les notions, qui n'ont aucun fondement dans la nature, à ces forêts du Nord dont les arbres n'ont point de racines. Il ne faut qu'un coup léger pour renverser toute une forêt d'arbres et d'idées. (*Interprétation*, fr. VIII, p. 185, my emphasis)

The term "notions" is first introduced in the preceding fragment VII where it signifies unsubstantiated opinion and contrasts explicitly as a product of individual bias ("notre," "nos") with "êtres extérieurs" ("Tant que les choses ne sont que dans notre entendement ce sont nos opinions; ce sont des *notions*, qui peuvent être vraies ou fausses"). In fragment VII, "notions" is curiously endowed with a material but negligible form. To illustrate the lack of substantive validity in those ideas without any basis in the material domain of nature, an image of rootless trees is evoked. As in the grounding metaphor of "notre terre" examined at the beginning of this chapter, it is from the perspective of a material realm of nature represented here by the metaphor of trees that "notions," like mathematics, are negatively informed. The lack of scientific substance, of "fondement," finds translation in this fragment in an allusion to the lack of "racines." Through this comparison with rootless trees, "notions" are from a textual perspective lent a visual, natural form that is depicted as vanishing before one's eyes. Any

---

9. See my discussion of the substitution of representation for writing in the first sentence of the *Interprétation*, ch. III.

"coup léger," any fact, can "renverser toute une forêt d'arbres et d'idées." In so doing, the trees would disappear, leaving a *tabula rasa*, a "tableau" emptied of its visible, seemingly tangible forms. Insistence on the importance of studying natural phenomena in conjunction with any particular philosophic/scientific "notion" or concept is played out in this textual enactment that grounds the abstractions of methodology, or language itself, in an image, which is a re-presentation of the material world. In conjunction with their role as the necessary cornerstone of experimental science, those "fondements" are also employed to represent their own lack, their own absence.

At the close of this same fragment VIII, Diderot introduces the importance of experimentation to the conceptual and reasoned study of nature.

> Cette liaison se fait ou par une chaîne ininterrompue de raisonnements, qui tient d'un bout à l'observation, et de l'autre à l'expérience; ou par une chaîne d'expériences dispersées d'espace en espace, entre des raisonnements, *comme* des poids sur la longueur d'un fil suspendu par ses deux extrémités. Sans ces *poids* le fil deviendrait le jouet de la moindre agitation qui se ferait dans l'air. (fr. VIII, p. 184, my emphasis)

The visual image of a thread held in place by the weights of experimentation conjures up, once again, a possible disappearance as it floats lightly about with the *poids* which secure it in view as well as, it can be said, without the weight lent by the image itself, locating theory of experimentation in the necessity of representation.

In the above passage, the simile is a vehicle employed to effect an adequation between a specific image and "être extérieurs" of nature. The textual relevance of simile here lies in the value of explicit comparison that points up a seemingly legitimate relationship, one of identity. The exclusively metaphorical value of "poids," like that earlier of "fondement" and "racines" is obscured by the fact that these entities resemble in themselves either the tools and instruments of measurement in experimentation, or the objects themselves of experimental study. Because of the evident similarity between these elements of the image and their virtual importance within a scientific study of nature, their value as rhetorical figures diminishes within the text of these fragments as they cover over their own poetic function.

Use of the terms "poids," "fondements," "racines" serve then several objectives. As part of the pictorial image, they secure the explicit object of vision, the "fil," the "arbres" and they also function to secure the very image represented. These are weighty metaphors of ground that are intended to ground metaphor in a comparison or simile whose explicit terms disappear before the "natural" image. In effect, the image of the forest would be swept out of sight as the string would be blown out of the frame of vision without such support as these very objects provide. Furthermore, "racines," "fondement" and "poids" act as metonymies for the entire visual image with relation to the more discursive parts of the text. It is the part that secures the whole, that subtends the linear view of trees, and the linear design of discourse.

A series of analogies have thus taken shape in fragment VIII: "raisonnements" are to experimentation, "notions" are to "êtres extérieurs" as "fil" is to "poids," as "les arbres du Nord" are to "fondement," and as discursive prose is to visual imagery; and finally, as the subject is to the object of inquiry. In each of the analogies, the second term is employed to supplement the first. Neither reasoning nor notions (stemming from the etymological root of knowledge) can prevail alone. Similarly, neither the thread nor the forest can remain within the field of vision without the weights, without the roots which anchor and sustain them. In each of these analogies, however, the second term supplements the lack in the first term and in fact is made to precede it. To valorize the concept outlined in the initial part of a fragment, or in a preceding fragment as was the case with fragments VII and VIII, the visual imagery introduced provides "substance" in retrospect for the initial principle. From the latter perspective only, however, is the first term ultimately informed in Diderot's text. Even within the pictorial representation itself of the thread with weights, the trees with roots, while it is the thread and trees which function as a focal point they both are made to depend on the second term which subtends them.

But this process of disjunction and assimilation of subject from and with object continues on a still more radical level in the tenth fragment. The oppositions senses/reflection and "hors soi"/"soi" of the preceding fragments reach an ultimate dichotomy in the relation now posited between nature and self:

> Mais par malheur, il est plus facile et plus court de se consulter soi que la nature. Aussi la raison est-elle portée à demeurer en elle-même, et l'instinct à se répandre au dehors. L'instinct va sans cesse regardant, goûtant, touchant, écoutant; et il y aurait peut-être plus de physique expérimentale à apprendre en étudiant les animaux qu'en suivant les cours d'un professeur. Il n'y a point de charlatanerie dans leurs procédés. Ils tendent à leur but, sans se soucier de ce qui les environne: s'ils nous surprennent, ce n'est point leur intention. (fr. X, p. 185)

Where "senses" were earlier validated as "hors soi," they are here fully informed with qualities specifically attributable to the external domain of nature. In fact, the "senses" of fragment IX as liaison with or potential metonymy for the objects of nature are exchanged in fragment X for "instinct." This transformation prepares an explicit shift from a perspective of the individual's perceptions to that of nature's activity in the appearance of the "animaux." "Instinct" is elaborated through an enumeration of the attributes of the senses. At the same time, a metamorphosis takes place by means of a personification of instinct as autonomous agents in nature: "L'instinct va sans cesse regardant, goûtant, touchant, écoutant." Such a description already anticipates the referent "animaux" of the second part of the sentence.

Both the conjunction "et" and the punctuation of a semi-colon underscore a connection between the two parts of the sentence and articulate a link between human instinct and the animals. This metonymical device continues to baffle clear distinctions of perspective. For once the attributes of "senses" slide into "instinct" as constitutive of the external world of the "animals," another distinction is introduced to allow for the now familiar movement through which those external entities as objects of observation will inform or rather transform the subject, the experimentalist.

To inform "senses" with the desired exteriority to "soi," instinct is made to inhere decisively in that which is external to the individual, almost contemporaneously with that movement which, through metonymy, has progressively linked such externality with the subject. At the precise moment a movement from "sens" to outside "soi" to "instinct" is to be identified with animals in the opposition sense/reflection, the phrase which accomplishes the transformation excludes the human subject. For with the assimilation of senses into the animal instincts, we are moving away from the implicit fusion of observer with the animal world. The experimental scientist is now posited with respect to a marked separation from the animals he turns out to be observing. Whereas the initial dichotomy of fragment IX distinguished elements of the same subject, "soi"/outside "soi," the classroom/nature opposition relocates instinct/reflection as two separate entities, animal/human. This distinction guarantees, in retrospect, the spontaneous, authentic activity of "instinct" precisely through its severed connection with the observer ("s'ils nous surprennent, ce n'est point leur intention"). In this way, human "instinct" is also contrasted to the preconceptions of any organizing principle conveyed here in the reference to the "charlatanerie" of the professor.

The metamorphosis of human senses into animal instinct is effected by a textual reversal which specifically excludes the observing subject from the newly instated perspective of the animals. This reversal is linguistically produced through a change in grammatical subject: from the observer who positions himself with respect to his object of study ("et il y aurait peut-être plus de physique expérimentale à apprendre en étudiant les animaux"), we pass gradually and definitively to the new subject of the animals. "Il n'y a point de charlatanerie dans leurs procédés. Ils tendent à leur but, sans se soucier de ce qui les environne: s'ils nous surprennent, ce n'est point leur intention." From the observer's perspective on the animals as his own object of perception, and which position is reflected in its grammatical place as objects of the verb "étudier," the former object "animals" shifts into the position of grammatical subject in the next sentence.

The grammatical shift operates decisively to exclude the observer so that, relegated to a place and a position external to nature's activities, he is represented as having no role in prescribing, in predicting, in construing before they come to pass, the instinctual movements of nature's creatures. Instinct, then, depends textually on the portrayal of the observer's role as one of response and of passivity, as a reaction which specifically does not coincide with the animals' actions or "intentions." The importance of "charlatanerie" as a practice of conjuring up a certain predetermined reality through tricks that deceive the viewer demonstrates a contrast with the lack of formative power and of authority in a subject who must succumb to nature's marvels, not preconceived, nor prejudged nor calculated to present or to represent a certain picture of reality.

And of course, in his exclusion from any process of prescribing the animals' actions, of knowing them in advance, the experimenter, the observer, responds instinctively, in surprise and even in astonishment. The very mark of the human subject's difference from the animals, his surprise at their particular behavior, is modeled on their characteristic of unpremeditated, unself-conscious, seemingly spontaneous response. Instinct, then, is to reason as animal is to human. And if instinct in Diderot's text both inheres in the material world of the animals and in the individual who perceives them, so animals mirror the image of man as his own difference.

If the creation of a field of scientific inquiry is articulated by the shifting thematic positions of the observing subject as well as by the changing place of the grammatical subject, such representations of nature that result function precisely to exclude the principle of the subject, to relegate the first-person, in chiasmatic fashion, to a position on the margins of that image of nature he has initially been employed to formulate. In this textual strategy, the observer defers to the action and image of nature which are shown to precede him. The distinction *nature/soi* that evolves in fragment X of the *Interprétation* parallels the contrast developed between writing and representation, "écrire" and "représenter" that we have discussed in chapter III. Both the relation of a descriptive or pictorial image to the discursive language that introduces it and the position of nature's observer with regard to a natural field of vision insist on the secondary and derivative importance of writing, language and theory. Those operations and products of the mind, be they observations, reflections, be they the tenets of experimental hypotheses, are defined in the text, as already noted earlier in this chapter, through comparison with the objects and tools used to perform those experiments and to "realize" abstractions. By their inherence in the natural or rather material world, these metaphors of the objects of experimental philosophy take on a consistency that conceptual language and formulae lack.

And yet, *De l'Interprétation de la nature* repeatedly qualifies experimental and methodological procedures in terms of specific models of writing. So in fragment X, the expanded opposition of instinct/reason is conceived in terms of authorship. The professor's relation to nature in his "cours de philosophie expérimentale" is negatively compared to the relation of an author to his own text.

> L'étonnement est le premier effet d'un grand phénomène: c'est à la philosophie à le dissiper. Ce dont il s'agit dans un cours de philosophie expérimentale c'est de renvoyer son auditeur plus instruit, et non plus stupéfait, s'enorgueillir des phénomènes de la nature, comme si l'on était soi-même auteur, c'est imiter la sottise d'un éditeur des *Essais*, qui ne pouvait entendre le nom de Montaigne sans rougir. (fr. X, pp. 185-88)

Through the previous reference to "surprendre" as an initial mark of difference/similarity between observer and animals, "étonnement," then "stupéfait" serve at the same time to widen the discrepancy between nature and the explicating professor. Instruction must in fact finally dissipate the observer's spontaneous reaction, his ignorance of nature. It is precisely with regard to the disjuncture of nature and man that the professor must instruct. To the extent such instruction claims to enlighten, this is the measure of distance to be established between nature's text and that of the professor's lesson.

The activity of explanation and reasoned instruction as a positive element in Diderot's methodology of science is then constituted by an interdiction against a certain kind of identification between the professor's authority and that of nature. For it is not only the student who should leave the lecture more educated and less amazed by nature's phenomena, the professor must take care in discoursing on nature's principles not to confuse the boundaries between these natural phenomena and his own authorial perspective. On the one hand, the very denial of the study of nature as an arbitrary, theoretical and linguistically abstract enterprise divorced from its referents is couched in the metaphor of Montaigne's text. And of course, we are not dealing here with just any text, but one specifically defined by the importance of first-person discourse—by its form of autobiographical writing. Here, as earlier, first-person discourse in the narrator's relation to his own text of the *Interprétation* is evoked only to be deferred, to be negated. Here as well, the definition of a professor's relation to nature is articulated on the interdiction of autobiography, and on the speaker's negative relation of authority and propriety to the text he is explicating.

The descriptions of the observer of the animals and the professor with respect to "philosophie expérimentale" follow a similar principle. The observer defers to the activity of the animals which finds expression grammatically, as already pointed out, in the shift to a new subject, "ils." In the latter case, the professor must, even as he instructs, defer to nature's phenomena, disavowing any authorial intentions. The professor's ordering of nature must not be confused with nature's own. And to that end, the instructor occupies a role of editor. It is Montaigne's text which must ultimately inform the work of Pierre Coste, as it must be the text of nature that must ultimately inform experimental philosophy. What belongs to the observer is formulated and exchanged according to what belongs to nature. Reason and knowledge in experimental philosophy can edit, but can only approximate nature's reason.

> Une grande leçon qu'on a souvent l'occasion de donner, c'est l'aveu de son insuffisance. Ne veut-il pas mieux se concilier la confiance des autres, par la sincérité d'un "je ne sais rien," que de balbutier des mots, et se faire pitié à soi-même, en s'efforçant de tout expliquer? Celui qui confesse librement qu'il ne sait pas ce qu'il ignore, me dispose à croire ce dont il entreprend de me rendre raison. (*Interprétation*, fr. X, p. 186)

This passage, in fact, mimes in its own syntax, the deferral of first-person discourse alluded to thematically by a reference to Montaigne's *Essais*. The professor's avowal of ignorance is initially posited in the words of the first-person "je n'en sais rien," then in the third, "Celui qui confesse librement. . . ." Earlier, the experimenting subject, first posited as the perspective from which nature is brought into focus, then acquiesces to a term external to his own sphere of organization. In this last sentence, "je" is instated in a position of negative authority as a precondition to being believed. The narrator then introduces himself into the discussion, taking up the perspective from his own point of view: "Celui qui confesse librement qu'il ne sait pas ce qu'il ignore me dispose à croire ce dont il entreprend de me rendre raison" (fr. X, p. 186). In his turn, the narrator now defers to the subject of authority which has become "il." "Je" acquiesces to the third-person so that "il" can now inform "je" (the narrator). " 'Je' est un autre" is made explicit in this ventriloquism effected by the narrator as he defers to a "je" specifically other. The writing "je" of Diderot's treatise, elsewhere as in this passage, relinquishes the very authority, propriety to which this pronoun would seem to entitle him. Nowhere is this more evident than in the dedication of *De l'Interprétation* where the narrator, also the authorial voice, changes registers from an imperious tone of the pedagogue to one of apparent effacement with regard to his readers. And curiously enough, the shadow of Montaigne's *Essais* continues here to play upon the writing subject.

The initial statement of the preface, "Aux Jeunes Gens qui se disposent à l'étude de la Philosophie Naturelle," followed by the command "tolle et legge," appears to set up the relation of author to reader in terms of teacher-student. This forceful position of authority is assumed, however, to be reversed in the subsequent passage:

> Jeune homme, prends et lis. Si tu peux aller jusqu'à la fin de cet ouvrage, tu ne seras pas incapable d'en entendre un meilleur. Comme je me suis moins proposé de t'instruire que de t'exercer, il m'importe peu que tu adoptes mes idées ou que tu les rejettes, pourvu qu'elles emploient toute ton attention. Un plus habile t'apprendra à connaître les forces de la nature; il me suffira de t'avoir fait essayer les tiennes. Adieu. (*Interprétation*, p. 174)

As in fragment X, the authority of the writing subject is undermined, this time with explicit emphasis on the relation of the author to his own text. Herbert Dieckmann's study, "Diderot et son lecteur," cites the dedication of the *Interprétation* as an example of Diderot's problem with his reading public.[10] Through his experience as editor of the *Encyclopédie*, Diderot came to accept a wider audience as opposed, maintains Dieckmann, to only his intimate friends and mistress for whom he clearly preferred to write. This critic then refers to "Jeune homme prends et lis" as an element of "condescension" and exclusion that persists in Diderot's attitude toward the reader. Diderot's precise reference to his targeted reader as "young man" did indeed cause Frederic II to desist from reading a book inappropriate for a "barbon."[11] Nevertheless, this dedication might be explained as a

10. Herbert Dieckmann, "Diderot et son lecteur," *Cinq Leçons, op. cit.,* pp. 15-41: "Des qu'il ne parlait plus au nom d'une idée de la communauté idéale des philosophes, il s'inquiétait de nouveau du lecteur. . . . Nous avons une première épreuve de ce que la substitution du 'genre humain' et de la postérité au public réel n'avait pas apporté une solution définitive, dans les *Pensées sur l'Interprétation* qui datent de 1753-54, c'est-à-dire après le Prospectus de *l'Encyclopédie*" (p. 31).

11. It is reported that Frederic II as well as others took objection to Diderot's dedication. The German monarch reputedly said: "Voilà un livre que je ne lirai pas. Il n'est pas fait pour moi qui suis un barbon" (ibid., p. 31).

need to initiate those just beginning to explore the paths of natural science: those as yet uncorrupted by the mathematical sciences and those who might be encouraged and challenged to undertake such an enterprise. Similar to Bacon's "true sons of science," Diderot's initial statement might be read more as a stimulus or goad to the uninitiated than as condescension towards or an exclusion of the general reading public.

But such speculation is far less important than the ambiguous status of instruction and authorship as conceived in this passage and as related to other examples throughout the *Interprétation*. Whatever the motive, the authority of the narrator is decisively attenuated in favor of the readers' own forces. If the initial statement to his reader introduces the dictum "tolle et legge," the paternal quality of this authorial command is effaced in the ensuing sentences.

The substitution of "exercer" for "instruire," of "essayer les tiennes" for "apprendre à connaître" provide the guidelines of this shift. The transitive process of relaying information from teacher to pupil is countered in the verb "t'exercer." Though a transitive verb taking a direct object, "je me suis proposé de t'exercer," the infinitive can also be understood in another semantic function. To the degree it is iden-tifiable as the pronominal and reflexive verb, "s'exercer," the object "te" becomes subject as well in this construction that can also be read in a reflexive mode. In the first instance, "je me suis proposé de t'exercer" can be understood according to *Robert* as "soumettre à un événement destiné à créer une aptitude ou une habitude." As a reflex-ive verb, "s'exercer" in the sense of "apprendre" in *Robert* is given "s'essayer" as a synonym. In effect, the shift from activity of the instructor-author to the pupil-reader becomes more explicit in the second sentence which revolves around the change from "un autre t'apprendra à connaître les forces de la nature" to "essayer," whose reflexive capacity is accented by the use of the possessive adjective at the statement's close: "Il me suffit de t'avoir fait essayer les *tiennes*" (my emphasis). A deferral to "un autre" who will bear direct informa-tion concerning nature to the reader, coupled with the emphasis on the reader's *own* forces, narrowly delimit the author's sphere of influence. In each of the sentences discussed above, an abdication takes effect which invokes the reader's activity to the detriment of the author's authority. Not only has the author-pedagogue denied any intention of providing direct, specific instruction to his young students, but in so doing the role of author undergoes transformation, becoming merely a mediator for the "essays" of the readers' "own forces." Those verbs so important in such a shift, "s'exercer," "s'essayer," are also clearly reminiscent of Montaigne's lexicon and the highly individual project of autobiographical activity in the *Essais*.[12]

But is this not an unusual use of both the terminology associated with Montaigne's lexicon and the project of self reflexivity central to autobiographical concerns? In minimizing his own authority, Diderot at the same time places the reflexive activity of "s'exercer" and "s'essayer" within the domain of the other—of the reader-student. The attributes that qualify the writing subject in autobiography have been extended by the author to his readers, thereby displacing both the authority and the reflexive subjectivity of the writing and narrating subject. What is gained by such an allusion to conventions of auto-biographical discourse in this context? One might point out that, while denying his ability to instruct the readers in the truths of nature,[13] he is, in fact, making a greater claim—that of substituting his text for nature itself. As a consequence of the disjuncture between author and authority, between the writing and autobiographical subjects, the text itself becomes, like the object of the experimentalist's investigation, a kind of testing ground by dint of its separation and distinction from any authorial intention or organization—the central focus for a field of natural inquiry.

12. A good example of the use of "s'essayer" can be seen in the following passage: "Si mon âme pouvoit prendre pied, je ne m'essayerois pas, je me résoudrois; elle est toujours en apprentissage et en espreuve" (Montaigne, *Essais*, ed. Maurice Rat [Paris: Garnier, 1962], II, 222).

13. Montaigne also makes a point of insisting that he does not teach others but rather recounts: "Je n'enseigne poinct, je raconte" (Montaigne, *Essais*, II, 224).

A short digression from *De l'Interprétation de la nature* to another work of Diderot, *l'Essai sur des Règnes de Claude et de Néron* will help to specify how first-person narration functions poetically to transform the notion of text into a metaphor of nature. Once again, we are dealing with Diderot's prefatory remarks to this *Essai*, which Jean Starobinski classified as an extreme example of Diderot's necessity to invoke "la parole des autres."[14] The *Essai* is conceived as a series of witnesses called upon to give reliable testimony concerning the events, actions and opinions which constitute the historical moment in question. Diderot describes himself as the mere collector of, as a respondent to, these testimonies of others: "Je ne compose point, je ne suis point auteur; je lis ou je converse, j'interroge ou je réponds."[15] Further on, in this same preface:

> Ce livre, si c'en est un, ressemble à mes promenades. Rencontre-je un beau point de vue? Je m'arrête, et j'en jouis. Je hâte ou je ralentis mes pas, selon la richesse ou la stérilité des sites: toujours conduit par ma rêverie, je n'ai d'autre soin que de prévenir le moment de ma lassitude. (*Essai*, Préface, pp. 1-10)

Diderot's reference to his book on analogy with promenades in nature focuses on the denial of authority and specifically authorship, consistent here with an emphasis on nature's own order and composition. It is precisely this denial that organizes and indeed constructs the foundations of history as so many concrete givens already previously set in place. Any preconceived project of the writing subject with regard to shaping the finished product of the text, which is also the product of history, is strategically eliminated by the conversion of history into the ground of nature, by the transformation of writing into "rêverie." As in our former discussion of the prefatory remarks of

14. Jean Starobinski, "Diderot et la parole des autres," *Critique*, 296 (1972), 3-22.

15. Diderot, "L'Essai sur les règnes de Claude et de Néron," *Œuvres complètes*, ed. Assézat (Paris: Garnier, 1875), III, 10.

the *Interprétation,* the narrator casts his very denial of authorship and authority in the rhetorical mould of autobiography. Of course, neither of the above examples can be strictly termed autobiographical in that the writing subject is not concerned with recounting his own story, his own life. Nevertheless, both the *Rêveries* of Rousseau and the *Essais* of Montaigne involve the process of studying a self that is posited rhetorically as already there—not created by and through the contrivances of the text. At one level, the "moi" is portrayed as already having its own history, secrets, its outlines previous to the task and/or the pleasure of deciphering and following its permutations and peregrinations. Diderot's use of autobiographical conventions in a text of history, in a work on experimental philosophy maintains this discrepancy in the service of an external principle of nature.

In chapter II, we discussed the parallel but different relation of author to authority revealed by Wilda Anderson's reading of Descartes' *Discours sur la méthode.*[16] Where method dominates in Descartes' discourse to usurp the authority of the author, Diderot's text subordinates method itself as it is related to the author's own procedure to a principle of textual representation. Diderot's text subordinates method to a principle of nature that functions as a metaphor for the text itself. And the modes of autobiography occupy a privileged position within this schema as a poetics enlisted to organize the external principle of experimental philosophy. Even in its subsequent negation, the narrating, authorial and at times autobiographical subjects are deployed to be reassumed, to be reformulated in the wake of a textual representation to which they have given rise.

The strategies of this poetics of nature that take root in the epistemological theories of experimental science are also, we will discover in chapter V, securely embedded in both linguistic and esthetic theory of the period.

---

16. Wilda Anderson, *op. cit.,* pp. 6-13. See my discussion of Anderson's analysis with regard to Bacon: ch. II, n. 6.

Chapter V
The Figures of "Inversion" in Language Theory and in *Lettre sur les Sourds et Muets*

The order of procedure is a principal element of any methodology of science, of any systematic philosophical thought. Methodology by definition must fashion a hierarchy of theoretical and practical concerns. Whether the method takes precedence over the individual's investigation and, as Bacon says, "lights the path and shows the way by it," or whether the experimental scientist plunges headlong into the dimly lit realm of nature's secrets seemingly forsaking method itself to the "natural" genius of individual exploration, an order of priorities remains integral to the project of science. Our reading of *De l'Interprétation de la nature* has demonstrated that questions of order and hierarchy constitute not only Diderot's explicit concern with a specific methodology of science but they are at issue in the rhetorical practices that constitute the language and the poetics of science.

As we have seen in chapter III, the question of an order of procedure in experimental philosophy is explicitly related in Diderot's text to the order of narration. Indeed, the order predicated by experimental philosophy seems to be homologous to that of discourse. We have found that the experimental philosopher like the first-person narrator, while taking precedence in the authoritative capacity of organizing the procedure, of governing the discourse of science, is subsequently demonstrated in the text to derive from and to depend on those elements he has supposedly introduced and engendered.

The textual patterns emerging in chapters II, III and IV emphasize the precedence of a second term in a sequence over the first. The experimenting and narrating subject as well as the organizing principle of the more discursive first part of a fragment as opposed to the predominance of image in the second part have in effect been shown to derive from what follows them in a textual sequence. These second terms indeed function in the text of the *Interprétation* as an authentic origin of the first terms. As we will see more precisely in this chapter, such a reversal interrupts the forward movement of narrative to a specific end, one that coincides with the concerns of mimesis in the close relation between eighteenth-century epistemology, linguistics and esthetics. Furthermore, the particular order we have discerned in the practice of experimental science, which is repeated in the order of narrative, is redundantly articulated within the smaller unit of the sentence. For a moment, let us return to the elaborate sentence discussed in chapter III which will serve once again as a paradigm.

Je laisserai les pensées se succéder sous ma plume, dans l'ordre même selon lequel les objets se sont offerts à ma réflexion; parce qu'elles n'en représenteront que mieux les mouvements et la marche de mon esprit. (*Interprétation*, fr. I, p. 177)

Though the narrating subject initiates the action of writing, on close analysis this sentence intimates a reversal of the order subject-verb-object. Within the established order of French syntax, an opposite order is repeatedly suggested, that of object-verb-subject: nature-action-experimenting, writing subject. Within the succession of clauses as they are read linearly, another reading is superimposed: "objets" would present themselves in the independent clause, preceding chronologically as well as logically and would inform the nominative case, consequently relegated to a position of subordination.

This sentence's order must be understood within a context much more specifically designated than either a rebellion against the rhetoric of traditional *dispositio*, as Peter France describes it,[1] or a Montaigne derived "nonchalance" with regard to style and subject matter, as Jerome Schwartz proposes.[2] Nor is it really a question of opposing or

1. Peter France, *Rhetoric and Truth in France: Descartes to Diderot* (Oxford University Press, 1942), p. 200.

2. Jerome Schwartz, *Diderot and Montaigne: The Essais and the Shaping of Diderot's Humanism* (Geneva: Droz, 1966), p. 121.

dispensing with order;[3] rather, it is a question, specifically, of reversing or inverting it. The publication of *De l'Interprétation de la nature* in 1753-54 coincides with a series of essays and articles on "inversion,"[4] which B.E.R.M. defines as follows in the *Encyclopédie*:

> Inversion: Terme de grammaire qui signifie renversement de l'ordre: ainsi toute inversion suppose un ordre primitif & fondamental; nul arrangement ne peut être appellé inversion que par rapport à cet ordre primitif.[5]

The eighteenth-century polemic concerning "inversion" in language theory poses specifically the question of the order of subject and object within the syntactical movement of a sentence. Chapter V will explore the opposing sides of this controversy with relation to Diderot's explicit and implicit stance on the issue. Not surprisingly, a

---

3. Herbert Josephs, *Diderot's Dialogue of Language and Gesture: Le Neveu de Rameau* (Columbus: Ohio State University Press, 1969), p. 98.

4. Charles Batteux, *Cours de Belles-Lettres distribué par Exercices*, V. 2: "Lettres sur la Phrase Françoise Comparée avec la Phrase Latine" (Paris, 1748). L'Abbé Pluche, *La Méchanique des Langues et l'Art de les Enseigner* (Paris, 1751). Denis Diderot, *Lettre sur les Sourds et Muets* (Paris, 1751). Du Marsais, art. on *Inversion*, Vol. III, in *Œuvres*, 4 vols. (Paris, 1797). Chompré, *Moyens sûrs d'apprendre facilement les Langues et Principalement la Langue Latine* (Paris, 1757). Condillac, *Essai sur l'Origine des Connaissances Humaines*, "Des Inversions," IIième partie, Ch. XII (Paris, 1746). Beauzée, *Grammaire Générale, ou Exposition Raisonnée des Eléments Nécessaires du langage pour servir de fondement à l'étude de toutes les langues*, 2 vols., V. II, Liv. III, Ch. IX, "De l'Ordre de la Phrase" (Paris, 1767). Batteux, *Nouvel Examen du Préjugé sur l'Inversion, pour servir de réponse à M. Beauzée, profess. de l'Ecole Militaire* (Paris, 1769).

5. B.E.R.M. is identified as Beauzée, a disciple of Du Marsais, who, at the death of the latter in 1756, was to take his place with the *Encyclopédie* as a writer of the articles on Grammar. In his article on *Inversion*, Beauzée identifies Batteux, Condillac and the then anonymous author of *Lettre sur les Sourds et Muets* as contenders of the "nouvelle doctrine" of inversion. Beauzée also mentions Pluche and Chompré (*op. cit.*) as basing their works concerning the teaching of grammar and language on these new principles of inversion. Beauzée's article in the *Encyclopédie* appeared in his *Grammaire Générale*, cited above.

two-fold movement can be traced. Diderot identifies two orders of language: the "institutional" order and the "natural" more "primitive" order of syntax. The distinguishing characteristic of Diderot's position, however, identifiable in his discussion of "inversion" as well as in his treatise on experimental science, is the insistence on both orders. The "natural" order of language, as previously, nature's own order, will be shown to found the inverse pattern. A "primitive" order of language will be seen to precede and to subtend the "reasoned," "institutional" order of discourse.

A polemic exists around the definition of the "primitive order" between, on the one hand, those *philosophes-grammairiens* Dumarsais and Beauzée, disciples of the school and grammar of Port-Royal and, on the other, Condillac, l'abbé Batteux and Diderot. What is the "natural," "primitive," "original" order of language against which "inversion" contrasts.[6]

Beauzée's "ordre primitif" refers to what he termed the "analytical," direct order of French syntax. "Primitive" in this capacity signifies, as in its etymological sense, a fundamental, a first order irreducible to something else. To the idea of the first, "primitive," or "natural" order Condillac brings an historical orientation. His "ordre naturel" refers to a language and mode of expression preceding the direct, syntactical order of modern French: a language of origins.[7]

Nous nous flattons que le Français a, sur les langues anciennes, l'avantage d'arranger les mots dans le discours, comme les idées s'arrangent d'elles-mêmes dans l'esprit; parce que nous nous imaginons que l'ordre le plus naturel demande qu'on fasse connoître le sujet dont on parle, avant d'indiquer ce qu'on en affirme; c'est à dire, que le verbe soit précédé de son nominatif et suivi de son régime. Cependant nous avons

6. For an excellent discussion of "inversion" with respect to the question of a mimetic theory, see Gérard Genette, "Blanc Bonnet versus Bonnet Blanc," *Mimologiques* (Paris: Seuil, 1976), pp. 183-227.

7. Etienne Bonnot de Condillac, *Essai,* pp. 247-52. See Genette's discussion of "langue originaire," p. 217.

vu que, dans l'origine des langues, la construction la plus naturelle exigeoit un ordre tout autre. (*L'Essai*, p. 247)

Those "objets" of the initial sentence of Diderot's treatise take the place of "je" in an order representative of the polemic concerning "inversion." The implications of "inversion" for language theory and for a theory of representation in Diderot's *Interprétation* necessitate a further study of the grammatical figure.

La *Grammaire générale et raisonnée* by Claude Lancelot and Antoine Arnault provided a basis as early as the seventeenth century for one of the positions in the eighteenth-century polemic. Du Marsais and Beauzée maintained the premises of their predecessors and endeavored to stave off opposition provided by those whose bias in language theory, as in philosophy, tended towards the natural, empirical sciences as opposed to a closed philosophical system, and towards history as opposed to a conception of universal reason.

For these grammarians of the Port-Royal persuasion the analytical order which presided over the organization of thought proclaimed subject-copulative verb-attribute as the "natural" one. Against this paradigm, "inversion," defined at the very end of the *Port-Royal Grammar*, occupies a very restricted area under the general rubric "Des figures de Construction."

Mais parce que les hommes suivent souvent plus le sens de leurs pensées, que les mots dont ils se servent pour les exprimer; et que souvent pour abréger ils retranchent quelque chose du discours; . . . ou qu'ils renversent *l'ordre naturel*. De là est venu qu'ils ont introduit quatre façons de parler, qu'on nomme figures, & qui sont comme autant d'*irregularitez* dans la Grammaire, quoy qu'elles soient quelque fois des perfections & des beautés dans la langue. (My emphasis)[8]

8. Claude Lancelot and Antoine Arnauld, *Grammaire Générale et Raisonnée* (Paris, 1660), repr. by the Scholar Press Ltd. (Menston, England, 1967), p. 145. Future reference to this work will be made in the text of this chapter according to the above edition.

"Inversion" belongs specifically to the "irregularitez" of grammar; it belongs to an order distinguished from that proper to the Port-Royal conception of language as reasoned organization. In fact, the last part of this section, also the last of Lancelot's and Arnault's book, vaunts the French language for its minimal use of figures in favor of clarity and precision.

> J'ajouteray seulement qu'il n'y a guère de langue qui use moins de ces figures que la nostre; parce qu'elle aime particulièrement la netteté, & à exprimer les choses autant qu'il se peut, dans l'ordre le plus naturel et le plus des-embarrassé, quoi qu'en mesme-temps elle ne cède à aucune en beauté ni en élégance. (*Grammaire raisonnée*, p. 145)

As the foremost disciple of Port-Royal in the age of the "philosophes-grammariens," Dumarsais spoke of "inversion" in a similar though more developed manner:

> La nature et la raison ne nous apprennent-ils pas: 1. qu'il faut être *avant* que d'opérer, prius est esse quam operare; 2. qu'il faut exister *avant* que de pouvoir être l'objet de l'action de l'autre; 3. enfin, qu'il faut avoir une existence réelle ou imaginée *avant* que de pouvoir être qualifiée. (Dumarsais, ch. VI, my emphasis)[9]

"Nature" in its approximation to "raison" in the above quote, emphasizes the compelling aspect of direct grammatical order. Theorists, such as Diderot, were to claim, also in the name of nature, that such an order was "artificial" and in some cases, arbitrary. However, use of the term "naturel" in its relation to "reasoned" direct order of syntax came into contradiction with Dumarsais' own notion of "constructions figurées" as discussed in his work, *Les Tropes*.[10] Dumarsais

---

9. Du Marsais, *Logique et Principes de Grammaire; ouvrages posthumes en partie, & en partie extraits de plusieurs traités qui ont déjà paru de cet auteur* (Paris: Drouet, 1769), p. 172.

10. Du Marsais-Fontanier, *Les Tropes*, publiées avec intro. de G. Genette (Geneva: Slatkine, 1967). Reference to this work will be given in my text.

followed the bias of Port-Royal, defining rhetorical figures as devia-
tions from natural order and expression. He gives them the term "idées
accessoires." However, these "accessories," not unlike Arnauld's term
"irregularitez," were also to be defined in the course of his work as the
most natural aspect of language.

> Il n'y a rien de si naturel, de si ordinaire & de si commun que les
> figures dans le langage des hommes. En éfet, je suis persuadé qu'il se
> fait plus de figures un jour de marché à la halle, qu'il ne s'en fait en
> plusieurs jours d'assemblées académiques. (*Tropes*, III, 16)

Dumarsais' inconsistency in this respect might be owing to a new
tendency taking effect which placed "natural" with regard to language on the opposite side of an ideal and universal reason.[11] As the
science of mathematics was putatively succeeded by natural science,
so in terms of language theory, and specifically with regard to "inversion," the ideal of a universal language based on reason gave way to
the differences of language based on a "nature" of history and imitation.[12] The interest in language accorded to their differences one from
the other was a component of the polemic concerning "inversion."
For, "L'inversion dans bien des langues faisait construire les phrases
d'une façon exactement contraire à l'ordre analytique."[13]

11. See Genette, "Bonnet Blanc, Blanc Bonnet," p. 211.

12. Gunnar Sahlin, *César Chesneau Du Marsais et son rôle dans l'évolution de la Grammaire Générale* (Paris: P.U.F., 1928), p. 85. Sahlin points to a seeming paradox in Du Marsais' use of the term "naturel" as "conforme à la raison" but which conception "ne correspond pas à la réalité." See also Genette's mention of this paradox (Preface to *Les Tropes*). It is interesting to note that Du Marsais' description of a "con-
struction figurée" (in the sense of sentence order) includes the same term "accessoires," as in his description of "tropes" as "idées accessoires." A "construction figurée" then is "celle où l'ordre et le procédé de l'analyse énonciative ne sont pas suivis" because of "la vivacité de l'imagination, l'empressement à faire connoître ce qu'on pense, le concours des idées accessoires, l'harmonie, le nombre, le rhythme etc." (Quoted from Sahlin, p. 83).

13. Franco Venturi, *La Jeunesse de Diderot*, p. 242.

Bacon's and Locke's influence helped to develop "l'idée d'une histoire naturelle de la langue rassemblant les faits sur différentes langues, étudiant les particularités et les rapports existant entre les différentes notions ou peuples et leurs moyens d'expression" (Venturi, pp. 242-43). Among the advocates of this latter viewpoint it comes as no surprise to find Diderot whose complaints against mathematics and a priori reasoning form much of the explicit thematics of the *Interprétation*.[14] "Inversion" as a grammatical ordering of language is inextricably related to a changing concept of "nature" as conceived in the domains of natural sciences and philosophy. An articulation of the opposing positions with regard to a theory of "inversion" necessarily implies contrasting uses of the concept of nature.

Inversion and Nature

The polemic can easily be grasped in Beauzée's article on "Inversion" in the *Encyclopédie*. The author reacts to the assault on the analytical order of language based on the principle of human reason; Beauzée makes an attempt to correlate reason with a "nature" threatening in the works of Batteux, Condillac, and Diderot to overrun or invert the concept of inversion itself:

14. In the school and often with the disciples of Port-Royal, not only are the differences overlooked from one language to another, but the principles of language are affirmed to be the same as those of all sciences, as those of the universal "esprit humain." Beauzée makes a very clear statement as to his criteria which I quote in full, owing to its paradigmatic status: "J'ai cru devoir traiter les principes du langage, comme on traite ceux de la physique, de la géometrie, ceux de toutes les sciences; parce que nous n'avons en effet qu'une logique, et que l'esprit humain, si je puis risquer cette expression, est nécessairement assujetti au même mécanisme, quelles que soient les matières qui l'occupent. . . . En suivant constamment cette méthode, j'ai trouvé partout les mêmes vues, les mêmes principes généraux, la même universalité dans les lois communes du langage; j'ai vu que les différences des langues, que les idiotismes ne sont que des aspects différents des principes généraux, ou des applications différentes des lois communes et fondamentales" (*Œuvres*, Vol. I, Préface, x).

Il n'y avait jusqu'ici qu'un langage sur l'inversion; . . . De nos jours M. l'abbé Batteux s'est élevé contre le sentiment universel, & a mis en avant une opinion, qui est exactement le contrepié de l'opinion commune; il donne pour ordre fondamental un autre ordre que celui qu'on avoit toujours regardé comme la règle originelle de toutes les langues: il déclare directement ordonnées des phrases où tout le monde croyait voir l'inversion; & il la voit lui, dans les tours que l'on avoit jugés les plus conformes à l'ordre primitif.

Reference to this "nouveau système" is accompanied in Beauzée's article by repeated attempts to situate analytical succession in word order as "ordinaire," "primitif," as inherent in "nature."[15] In fact, insistence on the term "nature" or "naturel" with regard to language augments in proportion to an explicit avowal of the disjunction between thought and language. The intrinsic difference between "parole" and "pensée" through "abstraction" leads Beauzée to designate "parole" in terms of its *own* properties—in terms of what is "natural" to its *own* mode of expression. Thought itself can not be represented faithfully in the image of the word: "la pensée est indivisible, & ne peut par conséquent être par elle-même l'objet immédiat d'aucune image."[16] Rather, it is "l'*analyse* de la pensée qui seule peut être figurée par la parole" (art. *Inversion*, my emphasis). Beauzée needs to find his way back to a concept of nature as necessary gauge of truth and order. Analytical succession of thoughts as informed by the metaphor of painting and a repetition of the term "nature" compensate then for the divorce effected between language and thought.

---

15. Beauzée makes reference to the "nouvelle doctrine," "nouvelle opinion" or "nouveau système" throughout the article. On Beauzée see Genette, p. 213.

16. Here is the quote in a more expanded form: "Mais la pensée est indivisible & ne peut par conséquent être par elle-même l'objet immédiat d'aucune image; il faut nécessairement recourir à l'abstraction & considérer l'une après l'autre les idées qui en font l'objet & leurs relations, c'est donc l'analyse de la pensée qui seule peut être figurée par la parole."

> Or il est de la *nature* de toute image de présenter fidellement son original; ainsi la *nature* de la parole exige qu'elle *peigne* exactement les idées objectives de la pensée et leurs relations. Ces relations supposent une succession dans leurs termes. . .: cette succession fondée sur leurs relations, est donc en effet l'objet *naturel* de l'image que la parole doit produire, & l'ordre analytique est l'ordre *naturel* qui doit servir de base à la syntaxe de toutes les langues. (art. *Inversion,* my emphasis)

The intricacy and repetition of the above passage is owing to Beauzée's definition of the order of syntax as both analytical *and* mimetic.[17] This second criterion, which features a translation of one medium "fidellement" into the next, from "pensée objective" to "parole," is best understood within the context of the opposition. From the perspectives of Batteux, Condillac and Diderot the new notion of "inversion" rests on the capability of language to imitate an order external to itself. Not only is language to be a faithful rendering of thought, thought itself is modeled on a close imitation of "choses."

> C'est de l'ordre et de l'arrangement des choses et de leurs parties que dépendent l'ordre et l'arrangement des pensées; et de l'ordre et de l'arrangement de la pensée que dépendent l'ordre et l'arrangement de l'expression.[18]

According to Batteux's hierarchy, any deviation from one register to another would be a reversal of the natural order. Diderot was to contend such a naive analogy between "chose," "pensée," and "parole" in his *Lettre sur les Sourds et Muets.* Nevertheless, while taking issue with a rather simplistic theory of language as imitation, Diderot was to refine Batteux's analysis. Within the context of analytical succession of discourse, Diderot was to retain the tenets of "inversion" as the traces, the vestiges of the "natural," "original" order of language.

17. See Genette, p. 213.
18. Batteux, *Cours de Belles-Lettres,* p. 301.

Inversion and the Tableau of Nature

Beauzée's mention of painting corresponds to a constant in the vocabulary and imagery of his opponents. The quality of analytic word order disrupted the integral "tableau de la nature" of which language should partake as a mirror image.

> Mais ce qui mérite le plus d'attention, c'est qu'en déshonorant ce récit par la marche de la langue francoyse qu'on lui a fait prendre, on a entièrement renversé l'ordre des choses qu'on y rapporte; & pour avoir égard au génie, ou plutôt à la pauvreté de nos langues vulgaires, on met en pièces le tableau de la nature.[19]

Association of "nature" with "tableau" is repeated consistently throughout Condillac's description of "inversion." Speaking of the advantages of "inversion" in either long periods or within shorter narrative statements, Condillac says:

> C'est qu'elles [les inversions] font un tableau, je veux dire qu'elles réunissent dans un seul mot les circonstances d'une action, en quelque sorte comme un peintre les réunit sur la toile; si elles les offroient l'une après l'autre, ce ne serait qu'un simple récit. (*Essais sur l'entendement humain*, p. 249)

The section devoted to "inversion" in Condillac's *Art d'écrire* begins with a reference to the writer as analogous to the painter. "Il est très utile en pareil cas [des inversions] de consulter le langage d'action qui est tout à la fois l'objet de l'écrivain et du peintre."[20] The word order of "inversion" corresponds in Condillac's explanation to the his-

---

19. Pluche, *Méchanique les Langues*, p. 115.

20. With the exception of the *Essai*, all other works of Condillac will be cited in the text according to the following edition with the title of the work and page number: Condillac, ed. Georges Le Roy, *Œuvres* in Corpus Général des Philosophes Français (Paris: P.U.F., 1947), "Art d'Ecrire," p. 577.

tory of man's development with regard to the use of signs. Inverting the movement of the accepted grammatical sentence privileges, on the epistemological level, the precedence of man's "original" expression with relation to the present, more analytical model.

> Les gestes, les mouvements du visage et les accens inarticulés, voilà monsieur, les premiers moyens que les hommes ont eus pour se communiquer leurs pensées. Le langage qui se forme avec ces signes, se nomme langage d'action. (Condillac, *Cours d'études*, I, 248)

Painting serves as the modern analogy of those principles inherent in the "langage d'action."

> Cependant si nous considérons qu'un peintre habile voit rapidement tout un tableau, et d'un clin d'œil y démêle une multitude de détails qui nous échappent, nous jugeons que des hommes qui ne parlent encore que le langage des idées simultanées, doivent se faire une habitude de voir, aussi d'un clin d'œil, presque tout ce qu'une action leur représente à la fois. (*Cours d'Etudes*, I, 430)

The simultaneous aspect of language, posited as the "original" and only "natural" way man both perceived and expressed himself, is reactivated by the use of "inversion." "Par cet artifice, toute la force d'une phrase, se réunit quelque fois dans le mot qui la termine" (Condillac, "Art d'écrire," p. 576). Diderot's introduction of the "tableau de l'âme" prefaces his discussion of the "hiéroglyphe" or "emblème" (*Lettre sur les Sourds*, p. 103). Simultaneity of "sensations" finds an analogy in the simultaneity worked through poetic, painterly, or musical inversion.

Batteux, in his discussion of inverted word order, emphasized a priority of the spoken word, "ordre oratoire," over the written word. Once again, the analogy of painting is employed in the service of a more concrete idiom:

> Nous cherchons l'ordre oratoire, l'ordre qui peint, l'ordre qui touche; &

nous disons que cet ordre doit être dans les récits le même que celui de la chose dont on fait le récit, et que dans le cas où il s'agit de persuader, de faire consentir l'auditeur à ce que nous lui disons. L'intérêt doit régler les rangs d'objets, & donner par conséquent les premières places aux mots qui contiennent l'objet le plus important. (Batteux, *Cours des Belles-Lettres*, p. 306)

Language breaks into the arena of "intérêt," bringing, through an attempted mimesis, a new concern with perspective. "L'ordre qui peint" is the "ordre qui touche." From "l'ordre analytique," invariable and impervious to "l'ordre des choses," the position from which the enunciator speaks with relation to an auditeur can reflect "l'ordre morale" (Batteux, ibid.).

The word order of "inversion" corresponds in Condillac's explanation to the chronology of man's development with regard to the use of signs. And a language which corresponds to such a precedence in history guarantees both the precedence of action, gesture, of the real, even the pictorial duplication of the real over the more abstract order of signs of the written language. What we are tracing here, with the above quotations from those authors of the "nouveau système" of "inversion," is the insistent approximation of writing to what is external to its own domain. Writing in its analogy with gesture, action, things or spoken sounds is a deferral of the written word as an abstract and artificial sign to the word as re-presentation. Within such a context, allusion to a previous age, an "original" moment in man's history, gives, nostalgically, a basis in chronological terms for man's reappropriation to the "physical," "material" realm from which language symbolically separates him.[21] Condillac's "langage d'action," like Diderot's

---

21. An interesting contrast to this perspective is Voltaire's position with regard to language, as interpreted in an article by Maureen O'Meara, "The *Taureau blanc* and the Activity of Language," *Voltaire Studies*, CXLVIII (1976), p. 162. Speaking of the action of the bull as representative of a primitive "language of gesture," O'Meara observes that "the actions of the bull can be seen to represent the primitive language of gesture that preceded words but lacked their precision. Voltaire feels no nostalgia for

"langage animal,"[22] ascribes to a reorientation of word and clause order in favor of the precedence of object or attribute over subject.

History and Hierarchy

The precedence of object over subject in sentence construction draws on Locke's and Condillac's epistemological theory. Development in thought moves from man's initial relation to the concrete to subsequent abstraction. Condillac develops Locke's schema within a historical context which situates primitive man in implicit analogy with the infant's developing understanding of the world about him.[23] "Cris inarticulés," "langage de gestes" draw on the response of an individual to the stimuli, to the object of his desire, fear, love, etc. Painting, poetry and music, in analogy with the past developments of man's history, become metaphors of man's contact with the concrete real of his primitive stages. For Condillac, Batteux and, as will be shown, for Diderot, reversal of the sentence order represents, then, a reversal of chronology.

As in the example of the initial sentences of the *Interprétation*, it is from the present or most recent moment in time that any narrator formulates an enunciation. But the sentence order, in its reliance on what came before or anterior to its own enunciation, both chronologically and mimetically, locates the present moment as a result, a consequence and a reaction to what preceded it. "Inversion," then, can be seen as an order which assimilates the past, the anterior. A priori reasoning of the subject from the present moment in discourse is suspended and

---

this stage and does not advocate a return to the language of action. For him, this language is inferior to a written or spoken form of communication and is a substitute acceptable only when man has not attained, or is deprived of verbal language."

22. See Paul Meyer, ed., *Lettre sur les Sourds et Muets*, Diderot Studies, Vol. IX, No. 196, p. 157. Reference to this work of Diderot in the text will be to this edition.

23. See Locke, *Essays Concerning Human Understanding*, III, Ch. I, Bk. IV. Condillac, *Essai*, II, Ch. 3, 7, 9.

replaced by an anteriority grounded in a history stressing continuity from object, from the third-person, the "non-personne," to the individual voice and perspective which ultimately articulates them as a response.

An Example of "Inversion" in "Lettre sur les Sourds et Muets"

Diderot's discussion of the development and use of the definite article stresses the aspect of anteriority essential to the concept of "inversion" as natural order. He places his hypothetical example in the formative period of man's linguistic development,

> où les adjectifs et les substantifs latins qui désignent les qualités sensibles des êtres & les différens individus de la nature, étaient presque tous inventés, mais où l'on n'avoit point encore d'expression pour ces vues fines et déliées de l'esprit dont la philosophie a même aujourd'hui tant de peine à marquer les différences. (*Lettre sur les Sourds*, p. 60)

Within this linguistic context, two men are situated according to their verbal descriptions of hunger—the difference between the two being that one "n'ait point d'aliment en vue, et dont l'autre soit au pied d'un arbre si élevé qu'il n'en puisse atteindre le fruit" (ibid.). The distinction resides in the presence of the object, "le beau fruit," likely to be placed as the initial utterance of one enunciator.

> Ainsi, quoi que ces deux hommes aient dit: "J'ai faim, je mangerois volontiers," il y avoit dans l'esprit de celui qui s'est écrié: "le beau fruit," *un retour* vers ce fruit, & l'on ne peut douter que si l'article "le" eut été inventé, il n'eût dit: "le beau fruit. j'ai faim. je mangerois volontiers icelui," ou "icelui je mangerois volontiers." L'article "le" ou icelui n'est dans cette occasion & dans toutes les semblables qu'un signe employé pour désigner le *retour de l'âme sur un objet* qui l'avoit *antérieurement* occupé; & l'invention de ce signe est, ce me semble, une preuve de la marche didactique de l'esprit. (*Lettre sur les Sourds*, p. 61, my emphasis)

Expression of hunger in this example is formulated in function of the object, "le beau fruit." Diderot's emphasis on a "retour" to the object of desire in the context of an already partially formalized language of linear succession demonstrates the following paradox: that it is precisely the notion of anteriority apparent in inversion of subject/object which occasions the development of language in the opposite direction as "la marche didactique de l'esprit." The article appears therefore as a sign of what on one level the "langage d'institution" is not: "l'ordre naturel." The article suggests and evokes the quality of "retour" specifically ascribed elsewhere, as here, to "l'ordre naturel."

The "marche didactique" can be understood in the above passage as an allusion to the progress of language towards a linear development which in its precision refers to, but is also a sign of, an original order. "Marche" speaks to the progress, the civilizing or institutionalizing movement toward the present status of the "langage philosophique," and, at the same time, Diderot represents the opposite: a movement ("marche") in reverse which effects a return ("retour") to an "original" source.[24] In such a manner, the grammatical necessity of referring to an antecedent corresponds as "trace" or "vestige" to the primitive era of "l'ordre naturel."

Another point of linguistic progress discussed with comparison to the "natural order" of the past can be seen in the example of the tenses. From his observation of the model "sourd et muet de naissance," Diderot affirms that the expression of time was among the last developments of language. He lists the order of invention of signs in language, the tenses of the verbs being the last included.

24. Meyer, ed., *Les Sourds*, p. 146. For Meyer, "la marche didactique" characterizes "une langue qui doit son développement aux études abstraites et philosophiques, par exemple, le français moderne." The term "marche" is used in the second sentence of the *Interprétation*: "elles n'en représenteront que mieux les mouvements et la marche de mon esprit." The suggested reversal of the first part of the sentence, where "objects" would precede the "thoughts of the writing subject," subtends the linear "marche de l'esprit" in the second part of the sentence. As discussed in my second chapter, however, the textual possibilities are more complicated.

Je peux encore ajouter que les signes des "temps" ou des portions de la durée ont été les derniers inventés. J'ai pensé que pendant des siècles entiers les hommes n'ont pas eu d'autres temps que le présent de l'indicatif ou de l'infinitif que les circonstances déterminoient à être tantôt un futur, tantôt un parfait. (*Lettre sur les Sourds*, pp. 55-56)

Certain languages, such as the "langue franque," "hebreu," "grecque" still manifest, according to Diderot, inaccuracy in their temporal distinctions. He takes these lacunae in the lingua franca and Hebrew, as well as the over-determination of the Greek aörist, as indices or vestiges of the earlier lack of temporal distinctions. The continuation of such pecularities into modern day usage finds a parallel in the sustained use of inversions according to a former, original order.

J'ai pensé que les inversions s'étoient introduites & conservées dans le langage, parce que les signes oratoires avoient été institués selon l'ordre des gestes, & qu'il étoit naturel qu'ils gardassent dans la phrase le rang que *le droit d'ainesse* leur avoit assigné. J'ai pensé que, par la même raison, l'abus des temps des verbes ayant dû subsisté, même après la formation complète des conjugaisons, les uns s'étoient absolument passées de certains temps. . . . Et que les autres avoient fait un double emploi du même temps, comme les Grecs, etc. (Ibid.)

Such examples of inadequacies as provided by tenses and due to a former, original order continue on in spite of progress and refinement of the initial, more crude idiom.

Je regarde ces bizarreries des temps comme des *restes* de l'imperfection originelle des langues, des *traces* de leur enfance, contre lesquelles le bon sens qui ne permet pas à la même expression de rendre des idées différentes eût vainement reclamé ses droits dans la suite. Le pli étoit pris & l'usage auroit fait taire le bon sens. (*Lettre sur les Sourds et Muets*, p. 57)

From the perspective of a progressive refinement of civilization and language these "traces" or "vestiges" linger on in what appears with this example as a negative aspect with regard to the instrumental prè-cision of the French language. However, this hybrid quality of lan-guage—as a composite deriving from the past forms which strangely persist within the present—allows Diderot to anchor once again such progress which has been achieved in French in a chronological evolu-tion. These "bizarreries" or "vestiges" nod to a return and to an initial model or prototype of the "natural" order of invention. In the same manner, with regard to the evolution of the species in the *Interpréta-tion*, Diderot harks back to the differences among the species, among the bizarre hybrids, to one model or prototype (*Interprétation*, fr. XII, pp. 186-88). Hebrew, Greek, the lingua franca are presented as lan-guage hybrids of one natural and original language of which French is, with respect to science and philosophy, the most evolved form.

From the critical discussion of Diderot's *Lettre sur les Sourds et Muets*, two separate and contradictory standards of inversion inevit-ably emerge.[25] On the one hand, following epistemological tenets con-cerning the formation and development of thought and language, the "natural order" of development of the sign in human discourse con-trasts with the French direct order of discourse. This "langage d'institu-tion," where subject precedes the verb and the object, is viewed in the light of the "natural order" as an inversion, thereby inverting the grammatical concept of inversion itself. On the other hand, the "langage d'institution" is accepted as the fundamental order of lan-guage, against which criteria Greek, Latin and Italian flourish in their possibility of syntactic inversion. From a reading of the *Lettre sur les Sourds et Muets* and, especially, from a textual reading of the *Interprétation*, the situation seems more complex. For, while it is true that Diderot enlists French as the language of science and philosophy and Greek, Latin and Italian as the languages of poetry, Diderot's own scientific prose shows a new blend or hybrid composition. Within the

---

25. Critical discussion of Diderot's *Lettre* usually involves at least two separate and contradictory notions of inversion. Hunt, in his article on this work of Diderot, sees three. H. J. Hunt, "Logic and Linguistics," *MLR*, XXXIII (1938), 215-33.

formal structure of "l'ordre d'institution," of subject-verb-object, of independent and dependent clauses, Diderot harks back, makes a "retour" to the "ordre naturel."[26]

According to Diderot, the "tissu d'hiéroglyphes" depicts a simultaneity which most specifically painting, music and poetry can render. This metaphor represents an initial and fundamental reaction of a subject to his biological ("tissu") and psychological environment. In this manner, "les choses sont dites et représentées à la fois." Painting, music and poetry double and derive from the "langage de gestes," from the "cris inarticulés" of primitive man in nature. Even within the structure of the "langage d'institution," within the syntactical order which initiates from the enunciating, experimenting subject, Diderot insists on retaining and evoking the "traces," the "vestiges" of another order, precedent to the explicator, an order upon which, in retrospect, the interpreter is shown to depend and from which he originates. A poetics of "les choses" can be glimpsed precisely within a chronology moving forward from the present moment of discourse, according to the grammatical situation of subject and object. If the present moment of the subject's enunciation is the initial point of departure through language, however, the chronology of the sentence's movement progresses forward grammatically while it regresses to a more primitive movement in time, to a more "substantial" and "objective" representa-

---

26. *La Lettre sur les Sourds et Muets* introduces the institutional order of language and the natural order of language first as categories under which French, Latin and Italian can be placed. But those two levels of language are also portrayed as existing within each one. This gives rise to Diderot's famous theory of poetic language. Says Genette: "On avait jusqu'ici une langue claire (le français) et des langues expressives (toutes les autres), voici maintenant que toute langue se divise en deux niveaux d'expression: celui qui suffit à la 'conversation familière' (clarté, pureté, précision) et au style de la chaire (choix des termes, nombre, harmonie), et celui qu'exige la poésie: alors, 'les choses sont dites et représentées tout à la fois. . . . Je pourrais dire en ce sens que toute poésie est emblématique' " (Genette, p. 205). My own contention would be that even before the digression into a theory of poetic language in *Lettre sur les Sourds*, Diderot has already alluded to the double aspect of the French language as both of the "institutional" and of the original "natural" order.

tion. Diderot's reference to "langage animal" as an equivalent to Condillac's "langage d'action" gives a specific emphasis on anteriority to the notion of precedence.[27]

In the elaboration of Fragment X of the *Interprétation,* concerning the modes of operation of the senses and reflection, a movement can be discerned which portrays such a "retour" to an earlier stage. From the point of view of the temporal present and an analytical, grammatical order the sentences move from subject, from scientist to object, from senses-instinct to perception of the object, animals; simultaneously, the reverse chronology is taking effect. For, as we move forward, cursively, grammatically, we are moving backwards to the elements from which human senses and instinct derive, the animals. From this chronology, which reproduces man's evolution, inversely, as though in a mirror, "reflection" and the language of the philosopher derive. From the point of view of the natural philosopher and narrator whose task must be to explicate from the present and from the evolved moment of a "langage d'institution," the deferral to instinct, to animals, allows him to become both a part of the evolutionary process as object and subject who through such a "retour" attempts to encompass his own difference as history.

It is not, therefore, solely within the realm of painting, music or poetry that "inversion" as "hiéroglyphe" or as imitation of the germination of concrete ideas takes place. "La chose même," ascribed to painting in the *Lettre sur les Sourds et Muets,* finds a parallel in Diderot's scientific prose through "inversion."[28] In this case, "inversion" solicits the "material," primitive moment of man's evolution through the grammar of civilization.

---

27. Meyer, p. 68. Meyer likens "langage animal" to Condillac's "langage d'action."
28. *Lettre sur les Sourds,* p. 102: "La peinture montre l'objet même, la poésie le décrit, la musique en excite à peine une idée." Also, "C'est la chose même que le peintre montre; les expressions du musicien et du poète n'en sont que des hiéroglyphes" (ibid.).

Science/Les Beaux Arts: Art/Nature

The analytic, direct order of syntax often alludes, then, to a precedent order. The temporal past, indicative of a preceding order, is evoked to prevail over the present act of enunciation; similarly, a representational image is shown to subtend and to precede a subsequent decomposition into a linear, cursive and more abstract language. The past tense of "les objets se sont offerts," in the second sentence of the *Interprétation*, can be extended in its function of paradigm to the thematic level of the historical past of man's evolution from the animals. In both examples, the introduction of "objets" and the presentation of animals come after the subject, in accordance with the discursive order of direct syntax and with the perspective of the observing scientist. Yet, both terms, "objets" and "animaux," take precedence over the present of the subject's enunciation and over the order of the direct and analytical language as such. Precedence as priority can also be understood in the manner such "objets" as the "abeilles," "les racines des arbres du Nord," and "les poids" subtend, even as textually they come after, the discursive aspect of a fragment or argument. These terms, all identifiable as pertaining to what is defined as exterior to the present of the enunciating subject are shown to precede chronologically and also to sustain the discourse of experimental philosophy and science. Such "traces" or "vestiges" of the former "real" order of objects as expression function as metaphors for "la chose même." We can extend our inquiry to a general question concerning Diderot's discourse of/on science. In the *Lettre sur les Sourds et Muets*, the French language was defined as the most evolved example of the "langage d'institution," in direct opposition to the "ordre naturel" of poetic language. It is therefore to the French language that befalls the honor as well as duty of sustaining and advancing the discourse of science and philosophy. But, according to our findings here, it would appear that the discourse of science is subtended and validated by what is explicitly other than the discourse of science.

Throughout Diderot's and Condillac's discussion of "inversion," as previously noted, the "beaux-arts," painting and poetry constitute the

metaphors for a language of the "ordre naturel." Such metaphors con-
tain the "traces" of "la chose même": painting mimes the simultaneity
of the "original" visual "langage d'action, de gestes," or Diderot's
"langage animal." Poetry appeals to the simultaneity of emotion and
sentiment, thereby miming the "primitive" spontaneity of "cris
inarticulés."

The textual manoeuvres at work in the *Interprétation* point to the
same necessity of a regressive, retrospective movement based on estab-
lishing a continuum proceeding from "la chose même," the "êtres
extérieurs" of nature, to the subject who must analyze and articulate
them. On a still further expanded level, then, the "langage d'institution" is to the "langage d'action" or "l'ordre naturel" as science or
"physique expérimentale" is to the "beaux-arts."

The initial fragments of the *Interprétation* inveigh against the
abstract metaphysics of the mathematicians. A condemnation of their
abstractions is accompanied by a complaint of the mathematician's
inability to appreciate "les beaux-arts."

> Et je dis: heureux le géomètre en qui une étude consommée des sciences
> abstraites n'aura point affaibli le goût des beaux-arts; à qui Horace et
> Tacite seront aussi familiers que Newton; qui saura découvrir les pro-
> priétés d'une courbe et sentir les beautés d'un poète. (*Interprétation*, fr.
> III, p. 180)

The opposition between mathematical expertise and esthetic appre-
ciation is not merely an allusion to the necessary well-rounded quality
of the "honnête homme." It is precisely the quality of abstraction
which prevents the mathematician from appreciating "les beautés d'un
poète." In effect, the scientific revolution of which Diderot speaks in
the subsequent fragment alludes to "les belles-lettres" in the same
breath as "la science expérimentale."

> Nous touchons au moment d'une grande révolution dans les sciences.
> Au penchant que les esprits me paraissent avoir à la morale, aux belles-
> lettres, à l'histoire de la nature, et à la physique expérimentale, j'oserais

presque assurer qu'avant qu'il soit cent ans, on ne comptera pas trois grands géomètres en Europe. (*Interprétation*, fr. IV, p. 180)

Experimental physics is grouped with fields of inquiry concerned all with concrete domains of man's activity and knowledge. "La morale," "les belles-lettres," as previously "les beaux-arts," help to qualify "la physique expérimentale" in terms of the mathematician's lack. In his discussion of the *Interprétation*, Jacques Chouillet points to the paradox of beginning a treatise on the interpretation of nature with a defense of "les belles-lettres": "C'est justement sur la défense des belles-lettres que s'ouvre, de façon paradoxale, *L'Interprétation de la Nature*."[29] In effect, Chouillet remarks on the relation between experimental science and the "beaux-arts" precisely along lines of a compensation or supplement to the rigorous but faulty philosophical system: "Il est piquant de voir les sciences dites de 'l'homme' s'aligner sur la science expérimentale, et le génie littéraire procurer à la philosophie rationnelle le moyen d'échapper au désastre des systèmes" (Chouillet, p. 331).

Chouillet comes very close to putting his finger on the compensating, supplementing aspect of "les beaux-arts" or "les belles-lettres" with relation to experimental physics. Aside from postulating in Diderot's esthetics a "unité d'esprit" analogous to Diderot's "unité de la nature," however, Chouillet does not pursue the paradoxical element involved. In effect, to the extent that the methodology of experimental science must declare itself not to be a rigorous, preconceived system but, rather, an effort to mime nature itself in its own explanation, the "beaux-arts" would appear a most likely model. Experimental science must be defined according to its similarity with what is other than the current scientific apparatus and according to what is similar to "la chose même" of nature.

The importance of "les beaux-arts" is not ancillary but lends sup-

---

29. Jacques Chouillet, *La Formation des idées esthétiques* (Paris: Colin, 1973), p. 339.

port to the new scientific orientation. The attempt to make language mime a preceding, more substantial "real" has involved, in the question of "inversion," a rupture with the direct order of syntax. It has often been pointed out that the diverse fragments of the *Interprétation* follow one another in no strict order indicative of a preorganized system of thought. Chouillet specifically discusses such discontinuity as Diderot's refusal of the Cartesian instrument of analysis. The textual ordering of the *Interprétation* should be viewed as a direct consequence of Diderot's opposition to the analytic logic of deduction— where one proof leads specifically or directly to another, where the second element of a series goes back to the first, is derived from the first.

> Toute la différence vient de ce que le discours du métaphysicien cartésien est censé reproduire cette continuité, non seulement par la rigueur de ses déductions, mais encore par l'aspect tautologique de ses enchaînements, de telle manière que les suites de ses raisonnements ne sont jamais qu'un retour aux vérités précédément démontrées. (Chouillet, p. 338)

This chapter has shown that the disposition of terms in a textual sequence often follows a pattern explicitly in contradiction to the above Cartesian model. For the most significant aspects of Diderot's discussion of method seem to be based on a metaphorical and extended use of "inversion." Within the direct order of syntax an opposite movement is taking place. The subject, though precisely the first term in a series, is made to depend on what follows, and not the contrary; for the second term in a series does not arise as the result of a deduction from the first. Rather, the second term is shown to have preceded and founded the first. For this reason, my own reading seemed to move retrospectively, elucidating the earlier (part of a) fragment from a position situated at the end or at the latter part of a sequence. As in the case cited in Chapter IV, it is ultimately from the perspective of "notre terre," the last entity of the sentence, that, in retrospect, the truth of mathematics' incapability can be understood.

A sense of rupture then often accompanies the linear reading of the fragments as also in the reading of a number of crucial propositions and phrases. The discussion of mathematics from the perspective of "notre terre" finds a corollary inversely, in the discussion of "physique expérimentale," from the perspective of "les beautés d'un poème," or from that of "les beaux-arts." If the "concrete" perspective of "notre terre" ultimately disqualifies the science of mathematics, the mimetic region of "les beaux-arts" serves to qualify "physique expérimentale." In the duplication of "les êtres extérieurs," "les beaux-arts" function as an intermediary between the hypothesized "chose même" and an articulation of the methodological principles of a science.

The direct analytical order of syntax was justified by the Port-Royal assimilation of the "natural" word order to Cartesian "raison" and logic.[30] The subsequent polemic concerning "inversion" as the "natural" order depended on a definition of "natural" in terms of an order of mimesis and history. Within such a context, it comes as no surprise to find in a treatise on the interpretation of nature the introduction of "les beaux-arts" which can precede, and which are a major constitutive element of "l'art expérimental."

As in Diderot's discussion in the *Lettre sur les Sourds et Muets* of the natural order of language in its contrast with the "langage d'institution," so the *Interprétation* can be viewed in terms of a parallel opposition between nature and science. With regard to the Cartesian system as well as to mathematics, science will always be but a poor imitation of "les choses." In a significant number of fragments, Diderot opposes, as shown above, the systems of rational thought to the nature of "les choses." Words are even explicitly viewed as abstract signs which make a poor substitute for a knowledge of external entities so that "Les mots se sont multipliés sans fin, et la connaissance des choses est restée en arrière" (*Interprétation*, fr. XVII, p. 190).

---

30. Following Genette, speaking of Beauzée, "Cette grammaire est la seule, de tout l'âge classique, dont le propos soit explicitement *cartésien*: 'J'ai suivi à l'égard de la grammaire générale la méthode d'examen proposée par Descartes pour toutes les matières philosophiques' " (cited by Genette, p. 212).

Experimental physics harks back to an order of representation of the object world as substantiated by the realm of "les beaux-arts." The arts are given positive value, however, as long as they function in a text to differentiate experimental physics from abstract science or philosophy. As the next chapter will elaborate, a contrast between art and nature must inevitably be drawn. Precisely because of the use and importance of mimesis as a level of representation integral to a science of the object world, a distinction must be secured between man's mere copy or reproduction of external reality and nature's own inimitable activity.

In the opposition art/nature the same mechanisms of exteriorization are at work as those studied previously: man's art must defer to and must be assimilated to nature's own process. An inquiry in chapter VI into the necessity for art to effect a more rigorous imitation of nature will lead from *De l'Interprétation de la nature* to a discussion of *Le Rêve de D'Alembert*. The rhetorical strategies of Diderot's fictional narrative claim a status in this work that purports to transcend the merely imitative function of art and to derive from nature through the process of materialism.

Chapter VI
Rêve de Pierre

The eighteenth-century concept of "inversion" as a principle of syntax ordering the minimal structure of a sentence has been demonstrated in chapter V to be expandable into a general textual principle of mimesis. As we review our investigation of *De l'Interprétation de la nature*, it becomes apparent with hindsight that the thematics and discourse of the experimental genius (ch. II), the strategy of the narrating subject (ch. III) and the definition and description of experimental philosophy with respect to the order of discursive writing and image within the fragment(s) (ch. IV), can in effect be seen to conform to an extended metaphorical notion of "inversion." Gérard Genette, as we have seen, relates this eighteenth-century concern to the attempt at a cratylian correspondence between words and things.[1] Diderot's language of experimental science is fashioned from a poetics designed to approximate nature's method and movements. For this reason, comparisons between nature and experimental art abound in the *Interprétation*, positing all the more adamantly nature's superior ability to the paltry attempts of art and man. While the text of both *De l'Interprétation* and, as we shall see, *Le Rêve de d'Alembert* attempt to instate nature as the model for the discipline of experimental art and science as well as for the art of creative sculpture, the description of nature itself afforded by each one, according to its representation in certain sites or according to its description as process is based on metaphor and, as we shall see, on myth.[2] The very opposition maintained then between art and nature, the very transformation and "inversion" of man's art into the founding gesture of natural process, is, in its turn, reelaborated in the textual figure of a chiasmus.

1. Genette, *Mimologiques*, pp. 183-226.
2. Diderot, *Le Rêve de D'Alembert*, ed. Jean Varloot (Paris: Les Editions Sociales, 1971). All reference to this work in the text will be to this edition.

A long conjecture in the *Interprétation* addresses the difference between art and nature. Man's work, unfavorably compared to that of nature's forces, should adhere in stricter fashion to the principle of imitation:

> Les productions de l'art seront communes, imparfaites et faibles, tant qu'on ne se proposera une imitation plus rigoureuse de la nature. La nature est opiniâtre. . . . La nature emploie des siècles à préparer grossièrement les métaux; l'art se propose de les perfectionner en un jour. La nature emploie des siècles à former les pierres précieuses, l'art prétend les contrefaire en un moment. (*Interprétation*, fr. XXXVII, p. 211)

A concept of time alien to man prevents him from such rigor. The "pierres précieuses" mentioned earlier in the fragment occupy an ambiguous position. They correspond to those stones made precious by the earth's laborious production; they can also allude to the jewels, gems and gold which alchemy and even chemistry try to "contrefaire."

> La nature est opiniâtre et lente dans ses opérations. S'agit-il d'éloigner, de rapprocher, d'unir, de diviser, d'amollir, de condenser, de durcir, de liquéfier, de dissoudre, d'assimiler, elle s'avance à son but par les degrés les plus insensibles. L'art, au contraire, se hâte, se fatigue et se relâche. (Ibid.)

The orientation of the physicist to a more direct contact with "les choses" leads him to the possibility of manipulating the raw materials of nature's abundance into new compounds. The comparison between man's and nature's production of stones and metals in the first reference leaves nature then to far outdistance man's capacities. The latter part of this fragment, however, instates a hypothetical creation situated at the level of man's capacities which would approach a closer imitation of nature.

> Qui est-ce qui est sorti des grottes d'Arcy, sans être convaincu, par la vitesse avec laquelle les stalactites s'y forment et s'y réparent, que ces

grottes se rempliront un jour et ne formeront plus qu'un solide immense? Où est le naturaliste qui, réfléchissant sur ce phénomène, n'ait pas conjecturé qu'en déterminant des eaux à se filtrer peu à peu à travers des terres et des rochers, dont les stillations seraient reçues dans des cavernes spacieuses, on ne parvint avec le temps à en former des carrières artificielles d'albâtre, de marbre et d'autres pierres, dont les qualités varieraient selon la nature des terres, des eaux et des rochers. (*Interprétation*, fr. XXXVII, p. 212)

From an initial allusion to the slow pace of nature's almost undiscernible revolutions, the second part of the fragment underscores the speed ("la vitesse") with which nature's objects seem to appear; and now it is the naturalist's formations which take shape in the unhurried time of his reflections ("réfléchissant sur ce phénomène"), "peu à peu" and following the exigencies of nature's temporal model, "avec le temps." The criteria for natural production in the first part of the fragment to which man's hasty and even frenetic ways are contrasted are seemingly inverted. The time of reflection, though not nature's time, seems to expand with the growing spaciousness of the caverns, producing artificial quarries whose formations compare favorably with nature's own precious stones and in fact rival her esthetic production. From the earlier reference to "pierres précieuses," the "albâtre . . . marbre et d'autres pierres" take shape now on the former model, set within the "terres," "eaux" and "rochers" provided by the naturalist's imagination. In his article, "Arcy," in the *Encyclopédie*, Diderot cites a description by a certain Demolet of the caves' stalagmites and stalactites:

Ces figures, ces pyramides, ne sont que des congélations, qui néanmoins ont *la beauté du marbre* et *la dureté de la pierre*; et qui exposées à l'air, ne perdent rien de ces qualités. (*Encyclopédie*, art. "Arcy," my emphasis)

The "marble" and the "stone" have undergone a transformation in the *Interprétation* from elements of description in the above passage, from their position as qualifiers in the text of "Arcy," to the hypothetical capability of the naturalist to effect such a process. It is on the textual model of transformation from simile to a literal project as referent that the "natural" transformation is to be effected. If the work of the naturalist derives from the model of nature's formation of stalactites, nature's model has been transformed according to an extension of its process onto a metaphorical and textual level. Though marble and alabaster quarries certainly did exist, their formation directed by man as a process similar to that of nature is an image, located neither in the perception nor in a hypothesis of man's experimental science, but rather in his imagination. The term "reverie" would indeed better suit this fragment as opposed to "conjecture."[3] Civilization's artistry is conceived on an imitation of nature as a metaphorical process that transforms the caverns into the "carrières artificielles" of Diderot's "tableau."

The last part of the fragment compares the projected creation no longer with nature but with "les grandes enterprises," the "tant de monuments" of the "goût antique."

> Mais à quoi servent ces vues sans le courage, la patience, le travail, les dépenses, le temps, et surtout ce goût antique pour les grandes entreprises dont il subsiste encore tant de monuments qui n'obtiennent de nous qu'une admiration froide et stérile? (*Interprétation*, fr. XXXVII, pp. 212-13)

It is ultimately with relation to the art of the ancients that the "carrières artificielles" are given form. The success of a scientific, technical venture, earlier compared unfavorably to nature's ability, draws strength from the model of the ancient's great monuments. The visual absence of a marble quarry formed by the drippings of grottos leads Diderot to indicate a model which is represented. As in the example of

---

3. As previously mentioned, Diderot used the term "rêverie" in place of conjecture in the 1753 edition of *De l'Interprétation de la Nature*.

"langage d'action" or the "langages de gestes" (see ch. V), the model is posited as the concrete literalization of man's expression in the past. The ambiguity of a merely metaphorical nature incites Diderot to resort to another "real" which, in this case, becomes another metaphor of the concrete, represented and thereby representable project of science, of "l'art expérimental" (*Interprétation*, fr. III, p. 180).

This conjecture describes an experimentalism which attempts a formulation in terms of its referent. If there must be an imitation of nature's own process, this imitation comes already derived from a textual interpretation of "la chose," from a metaphorized "naturel." To avoid a science which is constructed on man's systematic but abstract model, Diderot conjures up and conjectures an experimental science other than science and based on an impossible likeness with its object. Almost 100 years later, Baudelaire's poem "Rêve parisien" exchanges a natural paysage for "ce terrible paysage" of "rêverie" where "j'avais banni de ces spectacles/le végétal irregulier."[4] In its place, a "tableau" nonetheless reminiscent of Diderot's conjectured "carrières artificielles" displays "l'enivrante monotonie/Du métal, du marbre et de l'eau," in its divorce from nature, in contrast with and in war upon the mimesis Diderot wanted to realize. The "artificial" in Baudelaire's poem seeks to establish itself explicitly at the expense of nature's model. Diderot's lack, the possibility of eventually creating, recreating nature's model according to man's endeavor but always in avowed subservience to his model, becomes Baudelaire's gain: No longer "pierres précieuses" recognizable as the slow labor of nature, "C'étaient des pierres *inouies*,/Et des flots *magiques*" (my emphasis).

From the experimental scientist to the poet of post-romanticism, the nostalgia for the natural object and for the closure of the gap between the word, the "rêverie" and the natural world has disappeared. Baudelaire's "rêve" willfully vaunts its difference from the natural object and process. Within every strophe of this poem, either

---

4. Charles Baudelaire, *Les Fleurs du mal*, ed. Ernst Raynard (Paris: Garnier, 1958), pp. 167-69.

dominating as the independent clause or insistent in adjectival description, a tension is established between the elements of the natural world and the "rêve," "tableau," "génie" and "volonté," which fashion it "d'un feu personnel." Baudelaire insists on a rupture with the criterion of the imitation of nature to the advantage of personal "volonté," which exclusively determines the creation of his emphatically artificial, poetic landscape.

Through metaphor, Diderot transforms his "rêverie" into an artificial landscape founded on nature's model. Baudelaire, though concerned with expression of a state of personal vision exclusive of nature's process nevertheless formulates his personal "tableau" in terms of the natural objects of "métal, marbre, eau, pierreries." In a very important sense, Diderot's experimental science, modeled on "natural" substance and process, rejoins Baudelaire's poetics of the artificial:

> Le mouvement d'attraction et de répulsion envers l'objet naturel, inhérent dans le dualisme romantique qui se veut conscience mais qui conçoit l'être conscient à l'image de l'être chose, ce mouvement immédiatement vécu dans les contradictions font la richesse de Wordsworth ou de Baudelaire.[5]

The similarity of Diderot's "rêverie" and Baudelaire's "rêve" is pointed up in this parallel between a concept of mimesis functioning in Diderot's scientific treatise and a concept of language identified in late eighteenth and early ninteenth-century poetry. As developed in Chapter V of this study, Diderot's expanded use of "inversion" in the *interprétation* already approximated a rather precise concept of poetic language. It is no surprise then that the question posed by Paul de Man's article, "The Intentional Structure of the Romantic Image," coincides with a paradox our study has formulated with respect to

---

5. Paul de Man, "La Structure intentionnelle de l'image romantique," *Revue Internationale de la Philosophie*, 14 (1960), pp. 68-84.

Diderot's text: the scientific treatise introduced a hierarchy in which the concrete, natural object world prevails over the abstractions of mathematics, at the same time that it founds the writing subject, the experimental physicist, and the merely conventional linguistic quality of scientific discourse and theory.

According to de Man, a change toward the end of the eighteenth century in the importance and quality of the poetic image is reflected in the change of critical terminology. In the place of "fancy," the word "imagination" parallels a growing emphasis in poetry on object, on material substances. The substitution of a critical word whose significance lies in the value of its reproduction and imitative capacity finds analogy in literature, particularly poetry, in the following manner:

> Ce changement se manifeste par un retour au concret, un foisonnement d'objets naturels et terrestres ramenant dans le langage la substantialité matérielle qui l'avait abandonné durant les siècles précédents. (de Man, p. 68)

The profusion of natural objects which work their way to the center of poetic language, designating "un retour aux objets terrestres," is also indicative of a change in the structure of this language which, says de Man, "devient de plus en plus intensément métaphorique."

> Qui dit objet naturel dit présence immédiate de la matière et des éléments physiques; qui dit image dit, par définition, non-présence de l'objet. Il y a là une tension qui ne cesse de demeurer problématique. (de Man, p. 69)

A passage from Hölderlin's poem "Brot und Wein" serves de Man as a paradigm for the above paradox: "nun aber nennt er sein Liebster/ Nun, nun müssen dafur Worte, wie Blumen Enstehn" (5th strophy). That "words are born like flowers" emphasizes through the use of simile both the desired identity of words to flowers and the basic separation between them: "Contrairement aux mots, qui naissent comme une autre chose (comme des fleurs), les fleurs naissent comme elles-mêmes" (de Man, p. 71).

Transposed onto Diderot's conjecture, the same likeness and discrepancy can be perceived. The first part of the conjecture on the "caves d'Arcy" states the discrepancy between nature and man's ability to create. A plea for a more rigorous process of imitation suggests, however, the possibility of closing the gap between the production of man's science and that of nature. And as opposed to explicit technological or scientific knowledge, it is entirely on the principle of imitation that, in the second part of the fragment, the "carrières artificielles" are imagined. Even a technical knowledge of "le véritable moyen" which would shortcut nature's process of transformation is considered insufficient:

> Quand on posséderait le véritable moyen, ce ne serait pas assez; il faudrait encore savoir l'appliquer. On est dans l'erreur, si l'on imagine que, le produit de l'intensité de l'action multipliée par le temps de l'application étant le même, le résultat sera le même. (*Interprétation*, fr. XXXVII, p. 212)

The time of application for the production of marble and alabaster must imitate nature's process. "Il n'y a qu'une application graduée, lente et continue qui transforme" (p. 212). The constant of the principle of imitation defines the procedure of natural science in exclusive terms of nature, in terms of what it is not and can never be. As de Man states concerning the ability of the poetic word to found itself as a flower, and analogously, the ability of man's language of science to found itself as nature:

> Le langage poétique ne peut que naître; il est toujours constitutif, c'est-à-dire qu'il peut poser même ce qui n'est pas—mais de ce fait même, il demeure incapable de *fonder* ce qu'il pose, sinon en tant qu'intention de la conscience. (de Man, p. 74, my emphasis)[6]

---

6. It is interesting to note that de Man uses the term "fonder" in much the same manner Diderot uses the substantive "fondements" in *De l'Interprétation de la Nature* (fr. VIII, p. 185): "On peut comparer les notions, qui n'ont aucun *fondement* dans la

The perspective on imitation evoked with relation to poetry has indeed already been broached with regard to science in the seventeenth and eighteenth centuries. Bachelard provides us with a parallel in science to the literary intention of the text to found itself as "chose." According to Bachelard, certain tendencies of the "esprit scientifique," especially in the period which interests us here, articulated an understanding of nature in terms of empirical observation and experimentation, largely based on a principle of mimesis, on the "images" of the natural object world:

> En donnant une satisfaction immédiate à la curiosité, en multipliant les occasions de la curiosité, loin de favoriser la culture scientifique, on l'entrave. On remplace la connaissance par l'admiration, les idées par les images.[7]

In *La Formation de l'esprit scientifique*, Bachelard relegates the various images used to explain a natural process to attitudes and beliefs which he locates in a kind of collective unconscious. The consistent error of seventeenth- but especially eighteenth-century science was the way in which the image of an object, the reaction "sensible" to phenomena, stood in the way of scientific knowledge:

> La première expérience ou, pour parler plus exactement, l'observation première est toujours un premier obstacle pour la culture scientifique.

---

nature, à ces forêts du Nord dont les arbres n'ont point de racines. Il ne faut qu'un coup de vent, qu'un fait léger, pour renverser toute une forêt d'arbres et d'idées" (my emphasis). In both instances, the term is used to indicate the attempt of language to attain an imagery that is concrete and therefore successful in overcoming the abstract quality of words. Diderot's use of "fondements" speaks to the necessity of the image, which, as I have explained in Chapter IV, substitutes and stands in for the natural world which "grounds" the discourse of science. De Man shows how the very attempt at "founding" language as natural object, necessarily through metaphor, paradoxically evokes the very absence it intends to overcome.

7. Gaston Bachelard, *La Formation de l'esprit scientifique* (Paris: Vrin, 1938). Future reference to this work will appear in the text of this chapter.

En effet, cette observation première se présente avec un luxe d'images; elle est pittoresque, concrète, naturelle, facile. Il n'y a qu'à la décrire et à s'émerveiller. On croit alors la comprendre. Nous commencerons notre enquête en caractérisant cet obstacle et ne montrant qu'il y a rupture et non pas continuité entre l'observation et l'expérience. (Bachelard, p. 19)

The philosophical tenet underlying Bachelard's investigation and critique of scientific error can be formulated as the necessity to understand nature in spite of, or as he put it himself, "contre la Nature, contre ce qui est, en nous et hors de nous, l'impulsion et l'instruction de la Nature, contre l'enchaînement naturel, contre le fait coloré et divers" (Bachelard, p. 23). It is precisely in terms of a rupture with mimesis as a frame of reference that scientific knowledge can be attained; just as for de Man it is the explicit rupture of poetic intention with the mimetics of a concrete and physical world which, with Rousseau and Wordsworth, engenders a new kind of poetic authenticity (de Man, pp. 75-84).

Imitation of an external, material, concrete nature as the ultimate criterion for a scientific project as well as for a textual poetics can be examined at length in another "rêverie" of Diderot, *Le Rêve de D'Alembert*. The first "Entretien" of this work provides an example whose complexities surpass those of fragment XXXVII studied above; yet, the movement discerned in the *Interprétation* becomes more explicit in the "Entretien." Once again, the imitation to be effected involves, as with fragment XXXVII, the substance archetypical of the material, external domain of objects, that of stone. Similarly impervious to the passage of time and to human mortality, stone is also and consequently the most attractive matter for man to mould, and as we shall see, to shape in his own image.

In effect, the eighteenth-century materialist concern with the unity of nature involved the elaboration of theories and images based on the interrelation of the living organism with its extreme opposite, the inanimate object of stone. At the same time that the singular principle of movement and resistance of matter as a foundation for all animate/inanimate entities warranted the consistent parallel between man and stone, it will become increasingly evident that more is at stake in these comparisons than an exclusively scientific thesis. In a passage of one of the more extreme materialists, J. B. Robinet, the process of the formation of marble quarries is specifically linked to the internal process of the assimilation of food to living flesh.

> Un liquide circule dans l'intérieur du globe. Il se charge de parties terreuses, huileuses, sulfureuses, qu'il porte aux mines et aux carrières pour les alimenter, et hâter leur accroissement. Ces substances en effet sont converties en marbre, en plomb, en argent, comme la nourriture dans l'estomac de l'animal se change en sa propre chair.[8]

The process of assimilating nourishment into the living organism described in terms of a comparison with the formation of metals and stones in quarries and mines finds analogy in countless scientific treatises on the eighteenth century. Bachelard identifies the animist/ materialist complementary opposition between the external and internal processes as a common phenomenon. Furthermore, he points to a tendency among these "philosophes éloquents (du) grand Tout" (Bachelard, p. 177) to place more value on the internal as opposed to external process.

> Dans la Terre comme dans nos corps . . . pendant qu'au dehors tout se passe en décoration, ou tout au plus en opérations peu embarassantes, le dedans est occupé aux ouvrages les plus difficiles et les plus importants.[9]

---

8. J. B. Robinet, *De la Nature*, 3ième Edition, 4 vols. (Amsterdam, 1766), I, 18.
9. Cited by Bachelard, pp. 177-78. No further information given. Another example of the complementary opposition between the mechanisms of the internal/external can be seen in Buffon's description of the workings of the body: "Car les différences extérieures ne sont rien, en comparaison des différences intérieures: celles-ci sont les causes des autres qui n'en sont que les effets. L'intérieur, dans les êtres vivants, est le fond du dessein de la nature, c'est la forme constituante, c'est la vraie figure; l'extérieur n'est que la surface ou même la draperie."

The first "Entretien entre D'Alembert et Diderot" gives further witness to the analogy suggested above of the internal process of digestion with that of the earth's transformation and assimilation of stone. Yet, as further evidence of the materialist thesis, the comparison "la beauté *du marbre*" in the text of the article on "Arcy" of the *Encyclopédie*, gives way in the "Entretien" to a coherent passage linking one domain with the other. Diderot's text involves the stone's decomposition, which through the process of earth's destruction and assimilation, becomes in the text not metaphorically but literally continuous with human flesh and blood.

A necessity for a more rigorous imitation stated in fragment XXXVII initiates an opposition between the example of man's work and that of nature. In this later "rêve," however, man's work takes the specific form of a work of art, "le chef d'œuvre de Falconet." Such a product of man's genius is contrasted unfavorably with and eventually is also supplanted by the work of nature: the materialist animation of stone. In this dichotomy set up between a work of art and nature, the narrative seeks to identify itself with nature's process as opposed to artifact, thereby attempting to appropriate such "natural" process to the text. This emphasis will demonstrate in explicit manner what the fragment of the *Interprétation* implied. Claiming the work of nature as different and distant from Falconet's "chef d'œuvre," the interlocutor of the "Entretien" seeks through dialogue to incarnate the work of nature.

As in the example of the "Caves d'Arcy," the text advocates that man's production derive from a closer imitation of nature; however, as will become evident, the very "natural," "original" process defined in contrast to man's creation stems from a textual metaphor. The metaphor at work in the "Entretien" is the myth of the animated statue, Pygmalion. It is from the example of man's creation, his "chef d'œuvre," inferior to nature's process, that the natural process itself can be shown to derive. The operation of this myth throughout the text baffles the very opposition initially imposed between art and nature.

It is most surprising that in a text whose explicit scientific thematic relates to the animation of stone, the reference to "le chef d'œuvre de Falconet," most probably his "Pygmalion,"[10] has produced so little critical inquiry. Yet, specific allusion made by the interlocutor D'Alembert to "le chef d'œuvre de Falconet" has been repeatedly identified by commentators and critics as "Pygmalion aux pieds de sa statue qui s'anime."[11]

For these critics, probable allusion to the "Pygmalion" in the first "Entretien" serves exclusively as reference to a mythic prototype adaptable to the materialist concept of "sensibilité," to the thesis of the potential animation of all matter. Georges May points to Boureau-Deslandes who, already in 1742, had employed the Pygmalion story in the service of his "roman matérialiste": *Pygmalion, ou la Statue Animé.*[12] Condillac's *Traité des Sensations* is cited as another example of the animated statue thematic, utilized, says Aram Vartanian, as Condillac's central expository device.[13]

10. See the following: Jean Varloot, ed., *Le Rêve de D'Alembert*, Intro., p. cxxvii. See also, Varloot, p. 6, n. 2. *Diderot Studies*, XVII (1973), pp. 82, 84. Paul Vernière, ed., *Le Rêve de D'Alembert* (Paris: Didier, 1951), p. 9, n. 1.

11. Indeed, many indices confirm Falconet's introduction to fame as traceable to the exhibition of the "Pygmalion" in the Salon of 1763. No other work of this artist, Benot maintains, received the same unreserved acclaim as the "Pygmalion." Diderot responds to this work with a highly enthusiastic commentary in his *Salon de 1763*. He cites the statue elsewhere as a representative example of Falconet's art; and in a broader context, Diderot names the "Pygmalion" as a masterpiece of great sculpture in general. Vernière, *op. cit.*, p. 9, n. 1. Benot, ed., Diderot et Falconet, *Le Pour et le Contre: Correspondance polémique sur le respect de la postérité* (Paris: Editeurs Français Réunis, 1958), pp. 245-46. Diderot, *Salons*, ed., Seznec et Adhémar (Oxford: Clarendon Press, 1957), I, 245-47. Future reference to Diderot's commentary on Falconet's "Pygmalion" will be made in the text of this chapter. Benot, *op. cit.*, pp. 66-67. Diderot, *Salon de 1767*, Seznec, Adhémar, vol. III, "De la Manière," p. 337. Cf. also my article, "Metamorphosis and Metaphor in Diderot's *Rêve de D'Alembert*: Pygmalion Materialized," *Symposium* (Winter 1981-82), pp. 225-40.

12. Georges May, in *Diderot Studies*, spec. no. on "The *Rêve de D'Alembert*: Studies by Herbert Dieckmann, Georges May and Aram Vartanian," XVII (1973), 82-84. See the discussion there between Aram Vartanian and Georges May.

13. Aram Vartanian, *Diderot Studies*, XVII, p. 84.

Such examples of the Pygmalion or animated statue thematic, however, employed to the ends of a materialist exposition, have in effect precluded a study of the allusion to the "chef d'œuvre" of Falconet within the textual dynamics of the "Entretien." This situation is a consequence of a critical disposition, longstanding in French eighteenth-century studies, which separates fiction on the one hand from intellectual history on the other. Such compartmentalization which, in terms of a critical perspective, has implied two kinds of texts, persists in the critic's treatment of such a hybrid work as the *Rêve* where both fiction and the tenets of materialism are clearly operative. Within texts of this genre, a tendency to press literature into the service of ideas has produced the conflatable opposition form/ concept. The example of "le chef d'œuvre de Falconet" has been treated as the form which stands for the content of the materialist exposition.

In this respect, criticism has imitated the explicit thematics of the "Entretien." Recalling the circumstances which surround D'Alembert's allusion, "le chef d'œuvre de Falconet" is introduced into the text at the moment the interlocutor Diderot projects its destruction. D'Alembert's mention of the masterpiece occurs fleetingly in protest to Diderot's projected use of the statue for his experiment: to "rendre le marbre comestible." To demonstrate D'Alembert's formulation of the materialist thesis in extremis: "Il faut que la pierre sente," the pulveri- zation of marble, of Falconet's statue into "poudre impalpable," is the first step in the passage from the "sensibilité inerte" of stone to the animate "chair" of "sensibilité active."

The "chef d'œuvre" of sculpture is to be sacrificed on the altar of materialism. Similarly, a bias in intellectual history dissolves Falconet's masterpiece into the scientific counterpart of the materialist demon- stration. Such a convention which enlists the Pygmalion thematic as an exclusive signifier of the tenets of materialism is unresponsive there- fore to the textual opposition located between the sculpted masterpiece on the one hand and the materialist experiment on the other. Once ten- tatively identified as the "Pygmalion," Falconet's masterpiece is absorbed as a formal, literary image into the discussion of the passage from inanimate to animate matter. Yet, it is precisely in its destruction and seeming disappearance that this model of sculpture assumes textual significance. A thematic conversion of Falconet's work into an explication of the materialist process attempts to substitute nature's "original" work for that of imitative sculpture. In so doing, the text claims difference from a representational, mimetic work of art and attempts to found itself in the "real" of nature's text.

Explicit sacrifice of the artist's creation to an experiment involving nature's force of decomposition and assimilation involves an exchange of a unified and specific sculpted image for the "poudre impalpable" of marble becoming humus ("terre végétal"), "latus" or "légume" and, finally, the animated flesh of man. Falconet's masterpiece comes into play specifically to be displaced or subverted by nature's model which, as D'Alembert implies, surpasses the merely external imitation which is sculpture.

> Quelque ressemblance qu'il y ait entre la forme extérieure de l'homme et de la statue, il n'y a point de rapport entre leur organisation interne. Le ciseau du plus habile statuaire ne fait même pas un épiderme. ("Entretien," p. 5)

In its destruction and subsequent disappearance from the text, Falconet's masterpiece is converted into the masterpiece of nature's creation: the internal as external organization of animate, real flesh. Yet, the explicit difference from Falconet's work will take the shape of its negative model. The process which effects a transformation from the "pierre" of mere statue, even of Falconet's masterpiece, to the animate flesh of living man realizes in superlative manner the Pygmalion myth of animation. The disposition of these two movements suggests once again that of the rhetorical figure chiasmus. Nature's process has materialized Falconet's statue into real, not representative, animation. Yet, it will be demonstrated that it is the Pygmalion myth of animation which "materializes" as it represents nature's real, "original" process.

The denotation of "chef d'œuvre" is subverted here. For the very mark of originality, of its position as masterwork, comprehended in the notion of "chef d'œuvre," is, so to speak, turned on its head with the pulverization of the statue. The statue's destruction designates the sculpted "chef d'œuvre" as a copy, deferring to an original in the flesh. Falconet's statue is demoted to its rightful position as a second, an imitation of the first and original model of life. The amorphous form of fragmented marble, "poudre impalpable," assimilated by nature's process into the organization of man, will be shown, however, to descend textually from the model of Falconet's masterpiece. It is the art of sculpture which precedes and which shapes nature's process in its image.

In effect, the materialist formulation evokes the thematics of the animated statue even before mention of Falconet's masterpiece. Objecting to the traditional duality, "matière/sensibilité," the interlocutor Diderot introduces one substantive, "sensibilité," as the fundamental quality of all matter. Such a distinction is resolved into the minor, more accidental differences of the adjectives "inerte" and "active." As D'Alembert formulates it: "Ainsi, la statue n'a qu'une sensibilité inerte; et l'homme, l'animal, la plante même peut-être sont doués d'une sensibilité active" ("Entretien," p. 5).

This play of minimal differences, essential to the unity of the materialist thesis, finds a corollary in the very introduction of a statue. Why does D'Alembert's query concerning the "sensibilité" of stone change into the question of the "sensibilité" of a statue? D'Alembert's initial paradox in the first enunciation of the "Entretien": "Car enfin cette sensibilité . . . s'il est une qualité générale et essentielle de la matière, il faut que la pierre sente" ("Entretien," p. 3), becomes: "Je voudrais que vous me disiez quelle différence vous mettez entre l'homme et la statue" ("Entretien," p. 3). To explain the passage from "sensibilité inerte" to "sensibilité active" any "pierre" or "bloc de marbre" would have sufficed in the transformation from stone to human flesh and blood. As "sensibilité inerte" already suggests potential activity, the possible transformation into "sensibilité active," so D'Alembert's substitution of statue for stone already gives form to stone in the shape and image of man. What is specifically designated as not human, "la pierre," "le marbre," comes already shaped in his image.

The same relation of difference/similarity functions between "sensibilité inerte"/"sensibilité active" as between "la statue"/"l'homme," as between Falconet's masterpiece—the Pygmalion/and the animation of "real" flesh. The second term in each of the three analogous sets of oppositions, though explicitly posing a contrast to the first term, is nonetheless, shaped on the model of its difference. The materialist proposal of a "qualité générale essentielle à toute matière" necessitates the effacement of those differences it purports to encompass. The text proposes, proliferates, differences according to a similarity which is explicit from the outset. In the same manner, the destructive process and the decomposition of the mimetic sculpture is assimilated into the creative process and product of nature as narrated, and as appropriated, by the interlocutor Diderot.

In the relation "statue"/"homme," the natural object "pierre" has been replaced by a cultural artifact. Stone has undergone the sculptor's chisel to become statue. Subsequent mention of a specific artist, a specific statue, "le chef d'œuvre de Falconet," finds contrast in nature's anonymous forces. As in the above example, however, such contrast is undermined by a movement described by the agent and creator, Diderot. Referring to the passage from "sensibilité inerte" to "sensibilité active" in the act of eating, Diderot addresses D'Alembert:

> Oui, car en mangeant, que faites-vous? Vous levez les obstacles qui s'opposaient à la sensibilité active de l'aliment; vous l'assimilez avec vous-même; vous en faites de la chair; vous l'animalisez; vous la rendez sensible; et ce que vous exécutez sur un aliment, je l'exécuterai, quand il me plaira, sur le marbre. ("Entretien," pp. 5-6)

"Exécuter" intimates the destruction to be worked directly on Falconet's masterpiece at the same time as it alludes to an act of construction. "Exécuter un acte, un criminel, un ouvrage, une statue" was a common lexical entity as the article "exécuter" in the *Encyclopédie* testifies. Still another aspect of this verb is pertinent to its position in the above enunciation. According to *Robert*, "exécuter" in its absolute sense "s'oppose à concevoir, projeter" and approximates "agir; réaliser, acte." It is to this absolute sense of the verb that the text ministers. Insistence on a potential for realization, "je l'exécuterai quand il me plaira," prepares the subsequent verbal enactment in the present tense:

> Lorsque le bloc de marbre est réduit en poudre impalpable, je mêle cette poudre à l'humus ou terre végétale. Je les pétris ensemble. J'arrose le mélange. Je le laisse putrifier un an, deux ans, un siècle. Le temps ne me fait rien. Lorsque le tout s'est transformé en une matière à peu près homogène, en humus, savez-vous ce que je fais? ("Entretien," p. 6)

The form of the dialogue here concurs with the use of "exécution" in its absolute sense. Appropriation of language in the first person and in the present of enunciation transforms mere project into the acts of "exécuter."[14] The collapse of time, one year, two, a century, into the present moment of discourse gives shape and form to the anonymous temporal process of nature. In the return of marble to its origin in the earth, "je les pétris ensemble," the idiom of the sculptor is at work: "pétrir le marbre," to knead, to make it flexible to the artist's imprint; figuratively, to form, to shape. There is a consistent emphasis on the verbal acts of the enunciator: "je mêle," "je pétris," "j'arrose"; even the lack of action, i.e., leaving the "mélange" untouched for years, "je le laisse putréfier," is inscribed within nature's act of "execution,"

---

14. According to Benveniste, "énonciation" corresponds specifically to an execution, to an act of language: "L'énonciation est cette mise en fonctionnement de la langue par un acte individuel d'utilisation. . . . Il faut prendre garde à la condition spécifique de l'énonciation: c'est l'acte même de produire un énoncé et non le texte de l'énoncé qui est notre objet. Cet acte est le fait du locuteur qui mobilise la langue pour son compte. La relation du locuteur à la langue détermine les caractères linguistiques de l'énonciation. On doit l'envisager comme le fait du locuteur, qui prend la langue pour instrument, et dans les caractères linguistiques qui marquent cette relation" (*op. cit.*, II, 80).

through Diderot's act of enunciation. The reduction of the artist's masterpiece to fragmented marble, and its return to the earth and to nature's process reinstates, in pronounced terms, the agent and the artist. Furthermore, the process which disintegrates the substance of stone into earth evokes the term and process of petrification in the almost identical term, "je le laisse putréfier," thereby evoking the integral substance supposedly destroyed. Finally, Falconet's statue which, immediately preceding in the text, was to be the object of destruction, has disappeared at the crucial moment of "execution." In its place an anonymous "bloc de marbre" is placed into position so as to evoke and to imitate the sculptor's act of creation.

Responding to D'Alembert's puzzlement as to what happens after the transformation of marble into "humus," Diderot broaches the final step: "Il y a un moyen d'union, d'appropriation entre l'homme et moi, —un latus comme vous dirait le chimiste" ("Entretien," p. 7). Appropriation of marble, of earth by the digestive "moi" of the interlocutor, is analogous to the appropriation of nature's process by the language act of the enunciating speaker.[15] Diderot, interlocutor, has become the agent, the artist of his own animation, his own masterpiece: "J'y sème des pois, des fèves, des choux, d'autres plantes légumineuses. Les plantes se nourissent de la terre—et je *me* nourris des plantes" ("Entretien," p. 7, my emphasis).

In his commentary on Falconet's "Pygmalion" in the *Salon de 1763*, Diderot lavishes praise on the statue of Galatea: the marble appears soft enough to yield to impression (Seznec, Adhémar, eds., p. 245).

---

15. Benveniste: "En tant que réalisation individuelle, l'énonciation peut se définir, par rapport à la langue, comme un procès d' 'appropriation.' Le locuteur s'approprie l'appareil formel de la langue et il énonce sa position de locuteur par des indices spécifiques, d'une part, et au moyen de procédés accessoires, de l'autre" (ibid., p. 82).

For a discussion of "énonciation" as speech act with relation specifically to the use of pronouns and to the notion of subjectivity, also see Benveniste: "l'énonciation s'identifie avec l'acte même. Mais cette condition n'est pas donnée dans le sens du verbe; c'est la 'subjectivité' du discours qui la rend possible" (ibid., I, ch. XXI, "De la subjectivité dans la langue," pp. 265-66).

However, Diderot introduces the term "miracle" at the moment he describes the figure of Pygmalion:

> O Falconet, comment as-tu fait pour mettre dans un morceau de pierre blanche la surprise, la joie, l'amour fondus ensemble? Emule des dieux, s'ils ont animé la statue, tu en as renouvelé le miracle en animant le statuaire. (Seznec, Adhémar, eds., p. 246)

Diderot's emphasis on Pygmalion coincides with the official title of Falconet's work: "Pygmalion aux pieds de sa statue qui s'anime." The artist is designated by the proper noun whereas his creation receives the generic and possessive term, "sa statue." Galatea is relegated to the animation conferred by the gods and derived from ancient myth. As clearly illustrated in Diderot's commentary, Pygmalion unites in one figure both the animated and the animating, the sculpted and the sculpturing, a double, a replica of Falconet himself.

Diderot, the animated and the animating force of the "Entretien," the interlocutor and the author, sustains nature's process over the myth of artistic representation. Nature's process is textually represented, however, according to a myth of creation. Perhaps now the question can be answered as to why the proper noun "Pygmalion" was in fact omitted from the text of the "Entretien." The proper noun is prominent in the official title of Falconet's work but it is lacking in Diderot's text. The answer to this question of omission resides in the obvious way in which such an allusion would have indeed informed and contaminated the interlocutor Diderot's account of the contrasting and superior process of nature. To have mentioned the name of Pygmalion would have informed the model of nature's creative and "original" process with an artistic myth of representation. The omission of the proper name Pygmalion is related to the two other instances of disappearance of the "chef d'œuvre de Falconet."

Thematically, the introduction of Falconet's work coincides with the project of its destruction and disappearance into humus. On the semantic level of the text, the "chef d'œuvre" once more, at the moment of destruction, becomes the anonymous "bloc de marbre" so as to allow, as said above, for the approximation of the destructive act to the creative act of sculpture.

Such emphasis on disappearance relates to another issue which is fruitful to explore at this point: the question of posterity as developed in the correspondence between Diderot and Falconet.[16] Diderot's remark in the "Entretien" about Falconet's nonchalance concerning the projected destruction of his work, "Cela ne fait rien à Falconet. La statue est payée; et Falconet fait peu de cas de la considération présente, aucun de la considération à venir" ("Entretien," p. 6), relates directly to their polemic concerning the importance of the survival and judgment of a work of art for posterity. In effect, at the moment Diderot was editing the *Rêve de D'Alembert* he was preparing to put in order his correspondence with Falconet which had originally taken place from 1765 to September 1766.[17] At first glance, it might be asked why Diderot seems to oppose in the "Entretien" his own position sustained throughout the *Correspondance* regarding a belief in the survival of the art or sculpted object. As will be developed in the last part of this chapter, Diderot is working out his polemic with Falconet on another level.

The artist's "chef d'œuvre" proves dispensable in relation to its continuation in organic life and to the extent to which a "real" animation evolves in the time of posterity. The destruction of a merely imitative, sculpted form of life takes place as a transformation into living flesh and blood. One of Diderot's arguments concerning the importance of posterity as proposed in the correspondence with Falconet names the Pygmalion statue in a similar context:

Et que je puisse lire au fond de votre cœur, pourriez-vous me dire si,

16. *Correspondance*, to be found in Yves Benot, ed., *Le Pour et le Contre*.

17. According to Benot, "Dès 1765 une correspondance s'établit entre lui [Falconet] et Diderot sur 'le sentiment de l'immortalité ou le respect de la postérité' [Lettres à Sophie Volland, XI, 92]. Au moment même où il rédigeait *le Rêve* [ibid., XI, 223, 2 sept., 1769] il s'apprêtait à la mettre en ordre et à réfuter son dédain de la postérité et sa conception mercantile de l'art" (ibid., Intro.).

tandis que moi qui ne regretterois ni un Louis, ni 2 ni 3 (voilà mes
moyens) pour rendre *Pygmalion* et plusieurs de vos ouvrages à jamais
invulnérables par la main du Tems, vous ne donneriez pas, vous qui en
êtes le *père* et qui devez avoir des entrailles, un écu pour assurer la
même prérogative à ces précieux *enfans* là? (Benot, p. 38, my emphasis)

Throughout the letter and argument, Diderot alludes consistently
to the topos of the sculptor's paternity, of the sculptor's relation to
his works as a father to his own flesh and blood: "à des enfans de chair
et d'os. . . . Est-ce que tu n'es pas père? Est-ce que tes enfans ne sont
pas de chair?" (p. 38).

Without explicit connection of the "Pygmalion" to the animation
of stone, nevertheless, the proximity of the mention of the statue with
the insistence on Falconet's sculpture as living flesh and blood of its
creator appears in a recognizable textual frame. The "Entretien" begins
with a mention of the "Pygmalion" as "chef d'œuvre," proceeding
then, without further direct reference, to a discussion of the transformation of stone into animate flesh and blood of its creator. Not the
sculptor's art, it is the flesh and blood of a materialist process which is
celebrated as the continuation in posterity of nature's masterpiece.
Yet, as already discussed, the masterpiece of nature's creation lacks
not its creator. At the deeper level of the polemic with Falconet, as
understood in the "Entretien," lies a competition whose terms take the
form of the "ciseau" and the stylus, the works of sculpture and the
works of writing: "La pensée que j'écris, c'est moi. Le marbre que tu
animes, c'est toi" (Benot, p. 16).

If Falconet's statue represents the result of the transforming process
of art work into life, including the artist himself as a result of the
process, so Diderot's text molds the narrative of nature's transforming
process, inscribing Diderot-interlocutor in the act as in the product of
creation. An analogy can be traced between the simulated speech of
Diderot-interlocutor and the flesh and blood transformation which
overshadows the sculpted representation of life. The enunciating
speaker is to writing as flesh and blood are to stone. It will be seen in
the last part of this chapter that writing as speech, text as nature, claim

supremacy over sculpture and imitative art, elaborating a contrast already intimated by Diderot in the exchange with Falconet.

At a given moment in his polemic, Diderot seems to tire of stone and marble statues as the privileged signifiers of man's creation for posterity, of man's immortality: "Mais les grans noms sont maintenant à l'abri de ces ravages, et vous subsisterez éternellement ou dans un fragment de marbre, ou *plur sûrement encore* dans quelque-unes de nos lignes" (Benot, p. 54, my emphasis). Perhaps stone and the statue are indeed too susceptible to the passage of time and the corruption which comes with it. For, marble and stone do eventually succumb to the process of disintegration. Words and writing are impervious to such a process. And, as the process which continues the master work of nature, spanning centuries and including disintegration as part of its creative temporality, so writing erects itself as a natural "chef d'œuvre."

The narrator and interlocutor, Diderot, identifies himself with the time and process of nature not only as agent and manipulator but also as product of the transformational process described. At the level of discourse analysis, such duality can be ascribed to the hybrid quality of the dialogue itself. Though the "Entretien" is presented as a "mise en scène," as a dialogue form of a philosophical treatise, it bears attributes of both dialogue and narrative, of "discours" and "récit."[18] To a certain extent, it can be said that the "discours" appropriates in its own terms the narrative events presented. The sequence of events in the history of the passage from stone to humus to flesh would be considered the typical and, in this case, the archetypical material of the "récit," whereas insistence on those events from the perspective of the first-person located in the present of enunciation refocuses those events in radical fashion.

According to Gérard Genette's discussion of diegesis (*récit*) and

---

18. The distinction elaborated by Genette and many others between "discours" and "récit" was introduced by Emile Benveniste, *Problèmes de linguistique générale*, "Les relations de temps dans le verbe français" (Paris: Gallimard, 1966), I, 237-50.

mimesis (*genre dramatique*), based on Plato's and Aristotle's distinction,

> ces deux classifications [de Platon et d'Aristote] se rejoignent sur l'essentiel, c'est-à-dire l'opposition du dramatique et du narratif, le premier étant considéré par les deux philosophes comme plus pleinement imitatif que le second. (Genette, p. 52)[19]

Genette points out what both Plato and Aristotle failed to take into consideration: dialogue, in that words imitate words in tautological fashion, is not the most mimetic form, rather:

> Nous sommes conduits à cette conclusion inattendue, que le seul mode que connaisse la littérature en tant que représentation est le récit, équivalent verbal d'événements non verbaux et aussi d'événements verbaux sauf à s'effacer dans ce dernier cas devant une citation directe où s'abolit toute fonction représentative, à peu près comme un orateur judiciaire peut interrompre son discours pour laisser le tribunal examiner lui-même une pièce à conviction. La représentation littéraire, la "mimésis" des anciens, ce n'est donc pas le récit plus des "discours": c'est le récit, et seulement le récit. (Genette, p. 55)

In the example of Diderot's dialogue/*récit*, however, Genette's distinction is blurred. For if, on the one hand, the description of the passage from stone to animate life must be understood as direct discourse of the character-interlocutor Diderot, the events being presented take place in matter, in substance markedly different from the quality of words. The words of dialogue imitate what is explicitly external to the temporal as well as physical realm of a dialogical model. In such a manner, the incarnation of stone, the ingestion of nourishment into the living system, seeks a counterpart in the production of speech, in the execution of the speech act. These verbal acts of

---

19. Gérard Genette, *Figures II*, "Les frontières du récit" (Paris: Seuil, 1969), pp. 49-69. Reprinted in *L'Analyse du récit* (Paris: Seuil, 1981), pp. 158-69.

the enunciator effect more than a narrating of the process of animation. Consistent emphasis on the personal pronouns "vous" and, in this specific instance, "je," culminating in the reflexive, "je me nourris des plantes," imitates natural speech as proof of the animated substance of the accomplished process. The self-reflexive "je *me* nourris des plantes" derives importance from the speech act being accomplished contemporaneously with the signified animation of life. As the product and creator are fused together in the moment of creation—in which the "I" has extended itself through centuries—the act of speech not just accompanies but constitutes such a process, binding the natural process of "récit" to the substance and resonance of discourse, of self.

> Or, quelle est la substance signifiante (ce que les glossématiciens appellent "la substance d'expression") la plus propre à se produire ainsi comme le temps même? C'est le son, le son relevé de sa naturalité et lié au rapport à soi de l'esprit, de la psyché comme sujet pour soi et s'affectant soi-même, à savoir le son *animé*, le son phonique, la voix. (Derrida's emphasis)[20]

Diderot structures the written word so that it imitates animation through the device of dialogue which approximates speech. Writing vaunts its difference from itself, as from sculpture, imitating the passing of time through the narrative of event. And into this linear sequence simulated speech erupts as the animated sound and substance of presence.[21]

Our study of the "Entretien" has involved a series of dualities

---

20. Jacques Derrida, *Marges de la philosophie*, p. 103.

21. Jacques Derrida: "Si, pour Aristote, par exemple, 'les sons émis par la voix sont les symboles des états de l'âme et les mots écrits les symboles des mots émis par la voix' (*De l'Interprét.* I, 16, a3), c'est que la voix productrice des *premiers symboles*, a un rapport de proximité essentielle et immédiate avec l'âme. Productrice du premier signifiant, elle n'est pas un simple signifiant parmi d'autres. Elle signifie 'l'état d'âme' qui lui-même reflète ou réfléchit les choses par ressemblance naturelle." *De la grammatologie* (Paris: Minuit, 1967), pp. 21-22.

which are marked out in the text as oppositions between: stone/flesh and blood, art/nature, writing/speech. The movement of such oppositions as they have been demonstrated to work throughout the text consistently implies an attempt to assure their continuity. Writing, in the final analysis, of both the "Entretien" and the *Interprétation*, attempts to overcome its abstract, conventional status through the very means which insures its status: a metaphor of presence, of substance as in the "carrière artificielles de marbre," or as in the case of Pygmalion, a myth, a metaphor of creation. Pygmalion is not the only model of this last example.

D'Alembert opens the "Entretien" with an almost reluctant admission of the contradictions inherent in the attributes of a divine being and in a dualist conception of the universe:

> J'avoue qu'un être qui existe quelque part et qui ne correspond à aucun point de l'espace; un être qui est inétendu et qui occupe de l'étendue; qui est tout entier sous chaque partie de cette étendue; qui diffère essentiellement de la matière et qui lui est uni; qui la suit et qui la meut, sans se mouvoir; qui agit sur elle et qui subit toutes les vicissitudes . . . est difficile à admettre. ("Entretien," p. 3)

In the text of *Le Rêve de D'Alembert*, man has reassumed the contradictions of the divine being. The creator/created of materialism rivals a dualist conception of the universe, like Falconet's animation of Pygmalion, according to Diderot (*Salons*, I, 246), in emulation of the gods, as an "émule des dieux."

Conclusion

The present study has traced a movement across the demarcations of literary and intellectual history, thematic, linguistic and textual analysis. From the smallest entity of a sentence, to the level of thematics and to the broad spectrum of a discipline, and finally to the notion of language and writing itself, I have been tracing one singular mechanism at work in Diderot's texts. Whether it be the narrating subject within the structure of a sentence, the experimental subject within a fragment or the discipline of experimental physics as defined within the context of nature, these entities have been demonstrated to function within the texts of the *Interprétation*, *Le Rêve de D'Alembert* and *Lettre sur les Sourds et Muets* according to a dependence on what is designated as external to their own sphere or domain.

The concept of nature operates throughout this study as a principle of radical difference, being that to which each previously mentioned subject defers; the concept of the natural also operates as a principle of identity to the extent each of these entities is assimilated to, becomes its other. "Natural" language as defined in the polemic of "inversion" in Chapter V is to the language of "institution" in Diderot's texts as the physical object world is situated with relation to the experimental scientist and the narrating subject, and as speech or the portrayal of dialogue functions with respect to "récit" and, ultimately, to writing.

In all of these examples, a dichotomy formulated so as to define and thereby separate what is claimed to be an arbitrary, abstract or subjective perspective serves to evoke and to represent the object world and, simultaneously, to locate the text as integral to the natural process, to its own difference. Once defined as partaking of an external domain, the narrating "je" retrospectively registers the true order of "objects," the experimental scientist issues forth "résultats ignorés," experimental physics represents the object world as a function of an identification with the mimetics of the beaux-arts.

We have seen that in the above context the metaphor of the beaux-arts of painting and sculpture intercedes in the adequation of a language of science with the realm of nature. But what is the relation of painting, termed in the *Lettre sur les Sourds et Muets* "la chose même," to the visual, object world it duplicates? The mechanism of separation and difference operates, as the present study has demonstrated, to mediate the external, object world; some extension of this principle might then be found to operate in Diderot's art criticism.

In fact, it is precisely to such a movement that Michael Fried addresses his work on Diderot's *Salons* and eighteenth-century French painting and criticism in general. The principle of "absorption" proposed by this critic in his book, *Absorption and Theatricality, Painting and Beholder in the Age of Diderot*,[1] closely approximates one aspect of the duality I have outlined in the present study. According to Fried, Diderot advances such a principle as an explicit criterion for the aesthetic worth of a painting. "Absorption" entails, according to Fried, the attitude of extreme involvement assumed by the various characters depicted on a canvas. Either in single figure portraiture or in the group scenes often depicted by Greuze, these characters are shown to be completely absorbed in their respective activities. These figures are described in the text of Diderot's art criticism as totally absorbed in their activity to the exclusion of the beholder located, of course, outside the canvas. Following this perspective, painting can be seen as constituted by its difference with its own medium as a flat canvas, a work executed so as to be viewed by the beholder.

For the reader of the present study, such a situation is reminiscent of the description of the experimental scientist beholding nature. More specifically, a cursory examination of a passage already discussed in Chapter IV will serve to elaborate on the direction for future study of Diderot's *Salons*.

As the characters in a Greuze painting seem to Diderot oblivious to the front of the canvas and to the fact that they are being viewed as a spectacle by the beholder, so Diderot's beholder of nature, the experi-

---

1. Michael Fried, *Absorption and Theatricality, Painting and Beholder in the Age of Diderot* (Berkeley: University of California Press, 1980).

mental scientist, derives more from directly beholding nature than from a carefully prepared lesson of a professor:

> L'instinct va sans cesse regardant, goûtant, touchant, écoutant; et il y aurait peut-être plus de physique expérimentale à apprendre en étudiant les animaux, qu'en suivant les cours d'un professeur. Il n'y a point de charlatanerie dans leurs procédés. Ils tendent à leur but, sans se soucier, de ce qui les environne: s'ils nous surprennent, ce n'est point leur intention. (*Interprétation*, fr. X, p. 185)

The radical exclusion and separation of the beholder from the realm he observes is substantiated by a strategy which shifts emphasis from the viewing beholder to the actions, to the absorbed activity and obvious lack of persuasive intentions of the object, animals. Here, as in the *Salons*, exclusion and difference distinguish, through rhetorical and narratological devices, the observer from the observed, guaranteeing an authenticity, an "objectivity." Like fragment X, the *Salon* texts define the beholder's domain according to attributes which in their explicit difference from painting will then be employed to underscore the similarity of painting or sculpture with what lies external to the canvas or sculpted figure, with the beholder.

Yet, Fried's analysis of Diderot's *Salons* stops with the notion of exclusion of the beholding subject situated statically outside and external to the canvas. If the textual situation described in the *Interprétation* is analogous to the texts analyzed by Fried, then another survey of Diderot's *Salons* should provide evidence of an opposite and complementary movement.[2] For the experimental scientist is also, in the passage quoted above, portrayed not only as separate and excluded from the realm of the animals, he is defined in terms of his senses which are likened specifically to *animal* instinct: "L'instinct va sans cesse regardant, goûtant, touchant, écoutant." While the exclusion of

---

2. I have set out to do just this in my article, "The Art, Nature and Fiction of Diderot's Beholder," *Stanford French Review*, VIII (Fall 1984), 273-94.

a beholding subject takes effect at one level of the text, at another, he is assimilated to an external realm; he assumes the attributes of his own difference; he partakes of nature and of the painting as Other. In the same manner, "Lui" or *Le Neveu de Rameau* is described by "Moi," the philosophe: "Rien ne dissemble plus de lui que lui-même."[3]

Studies have underscored the movement of *Le Neveu de Rameau*, of "Lui" as a principle of radical exteriority and difference. The present study elaborates, however, a similar principle of exteriorization and difference beyond a specific narrative voice and beyond the specific genre of fiction. The presentation of the narrating "je" and the experimental scientist of the *Interprétation* as well as the presentation of the discipline itself of experimental physics have all demonstrated a similar principle: these entities are defined in the text by what this text simultaneously demonstrates they are not. Experimental physics, then, has been shown to dwell under the aegis of the "neveu."

By locating this principle within Diderot's treatise on methodology of science a reading of the *Interprétation* necessarily raises a question as to the notion of empirical natural sciences as they developed and as they were described in other texts of the eighteenth century. Numerous historians have labeled Diderot's treatise as an emblem and as a herald of the new era of empirical and experimental science and thought. As my argument has sustained, however, the notion of experimental science as portrayed in the *Interprétation* consistently implies in its notion of "objet," of "objectivity," a highly metaphorical and even, in *Le Rêve de D'Alembert*, a mythical notion of nature and the natural.

To the extent a treatise on experimental science has been shown to accommodate and to derive from a theory of representation implied in the mimetics of the beaux-arts and in the principle of "inversion," the empirical tenets of natural science should be reviewed and reexamined in other texts of the period. Chapters I and II identify in cursory manner some similar formulations to be found in the work of Locke and

---

3. Diderot, *Œuvres romanesques* (Paris: Garnier, 1962), p. 396.

Buffon. Such a broad study of empirical and experimental science as defined in the texts of the period, however, must be the task of another inquiry. Suffice it to say here that within Diderot's works the *Interprétation*, though identified as a locus of an important event in the history of ideas, has also been identified in this study as the locus of a principle operating seemingly at odds with empirical scientific concerns and in tandem with strategies of fiction in the eighteenth century.

Diderot carries to an extreme a tendency, even a mania, in eighteenth-century thought to classify all the various and different branches of the human and natural sciences and to assert their interdependence. Like Bacon's tree of knowledge emblematically placed at the beginning of the *Encyclopédie*, these different branches of knowledge and thought, however disparate, are ultimately considered to stem from and to constitute the unifying concept of Nature.

In the name of different concepts, modern criticism also endeavors to reconsider the human sciences across existing demarcations which since the nineteenth century separate philosophy from a fictional rhetoric or science from literature. The all-subsuming concept and metaphor of Nature has been replaced in the twentieth century with new models, perhaps the most important of which is the model of language.

This study has provided an example of the disappearing distinction between the text of philosophy/science as speaking a language of truth and literature as speaking a language of fiction. In tracing Diderot's poetics through rhetorical devices which insist on cutting across distinctions of discipline and genre, the modern critic recognizes, as (s)he reflects, a strangely familiar context.

Bibliography

A. Consulted Editions of Diderot's Works

Diderot, Denis. *Correspondance*. Ed. Georges Roth and Jean Varloot. Paris: Editions de Minuit, 1955-1970. Vols. I-IX.

_____. *De l'Interprétation de la nature*. Photocopy. Paris, 1753.

_____ and Falconet. *Le Pour et Le Contre: Correspondance polémique sur le respect de la postérité, Pline et les anciens*. Ed. Yves Benot. Paris: Editeurs Français Réunis, 1958.

_____ and Jean D'Alembert. *Encyclopédie, ou Dictionnaire raisonné des sciences, des arts et des métiers*. 36 vols. Berne and Lausanne: Société typographique, 1780. Vols. I, II, III, IX, XII, XVI, XVIII, XIX.

_____. *Lettre sur les Sourds et Muets*. Ed. Paul Meyer. *Diderot Studies*. Vol. VIII. Geneva: Droz, 1965.

_____. *Œuvres*. Ed. André Billy. Paris: Pléiade, 1946.

_____. *Œuvres*. Ed. Assézat and Tourneux. 20 vols. Paris: Garnier, 1876.

_____. *Œuvres esthétiques*. Ed. Paul Vernière. Paris: Garnier, 1968.

_____. *Œuvres philosophiques*. Ed. Paul Vernière. Paris: Garnier, 1964.

_____. *Œuvres romanesques*. Ed. Henri Bénac. Paris: Garnier, 1962.

_____. *Le Rêve de D'Alembert*. Ed. Jean Varloot. Paris: Les Editions Sociales, 1962, 1971.

_____. *Le Rêve de D'Alembert*. Ed. Paul Vernière. Paris: Didier, 1951.

_____. *Les Salons*. Ed. Jean Seznec et Jean Adhémar. Oxford: Clarendon Press, 1957-67. 4 vols.

B. Consulted Works Up To and Including Works of the Eighteenth Century

Bacon, Francis. "Novum Organum," *The Works of Francis Bacon*. Ed. J. Spedding, R. L. Ellis, D. D. Heath. London: Longmans & Co., 1857-74. Vols. I, VIII.

Batteux, Charles. "Lettres sur la Phrase Françoise Comparée avec la Phrase Latine," *Cours de Belles-Lettres distribué par Exercises*. Paris: n.p., 1947. Vol. II.

_____. *Nouvel Examen du Préjugé sur l'Inversion, pour servir de réponse à M. Beauzée, professeur de l'Ecole Militaire*. Paris: n.p., 1767.

Beauzée, Nicolas. *Grammaire Générale, ou Exposition Raisonnée des Eléments Nécessaires du langage pour servir de fondement à l'étude de toutes les Langues*. 2 vols. Paris: n.p., 1767. Rpt. Ed. B. E. Bartlett. The Hague: Mouton, 1975.

Boureau-Deslandes, André-François. *Receuil de différents traités de Physique Naturelle propre à perfectionner ces deux sciences*. Paris: Quillau, 1748.

_____. *Pigmalion ou La Statue Animée*. Londres: S. Harding, 1741. Rept. in Geissler

Rolf. *Boureau-Deslandes: Ein Materialist der Fruhanfklarung.* Berlin: Rutten & Loening, 1967. 117-46.

Buffon, Georges Leclerc de. *Œuvres complètes.* Paris: Imprimerie Royale, 1774-1779. Rept. Paris: Ladrance and Verdière, 1830. Vols. I, III.

Chompré, Pierre. *Moyens sûrs d'apprendre facilement les Langues et Principalement La Latine.* Paris: n.p., 1757.

Condillac, Etienne Bonnot de. *Essai sur l'Origine des Connaissances Humaines.* Preceded by "l'Archéologie du Frivole," Jacques Derrida. Ed. C. Porset. Paris: Galilée, 1973.

_____. *Œuvres.* Ed. Georges le Roy. Corpus Général des Philosophes Français. 3 vols. Paris: Presses Universitaires de France, 1947-1951. Vols. I, II.

Dumarsais, César Chesneau. "Abstraction." In *Encyclopédie, ou Dictionnaire raisonné des sciences, des arts et des métiers.* Denis Diderot et Jean D'Alembert. Berne et Lausanne: Société typographique, 1780. Vol. I.

_____. "Exposition d'une méthode raisonnée pour apprendre la langue Latine." In *Œuvres.* Paris: n.p., 1772. Rept. Paris: n.p., 1797. Vol. I.

_____. "Inversion." In *Œuvres.* Paris: n.p., 1772. Rept. Paris: n.p., 1797. Vol. III.

_____. *Logique et Principes de Grammaire; ouvrages posthumes en partie, & en partie extraits de plusieurs traités qui ont déjà parus de cet auteur.* Paris: Drouet, 1769.

_____. *La Logique; ou, les premiers développements de l'Art de Penser.* Geneva: n.p., 1785.

_____ and Pierre Fontanier. *Les Tropes.* 2 vols. Paris: 1818; facsimile rept. Introduction G. Genette. Geneva: Slatkine, 1967.

Lancelot, Claude and Antoine Arnault. *Grammaire Générale et Raisonnée.* Paris, 1660; facsimile rept. Menston, England: The Scholar Press Ltd., 1967.

Locke, John. *An Essay Concerning Human Understanding.* Ed. A. C. Fraser. 2 vols. New York: Dover, 1959.

Montaigne, Michel de. *Essais.* Ed. Maurice Rat. Paris: Garnier, 1962. Vol. 2.

Pluche, Noël Antoine. *La Méchanique des Langues et l'Art de les Enseigner.* Paris: n.p., 1751.

Robinet, J. B. *De la Nature.* 3ième ed., 4 vols. Amsterdam, n.p., 1766.

C. Critical Works

Aarsleff, Hans. *From Locke to Saussure.* Minneapolis: University of Minnesota Press, 1982.

Anderson, Wilda. *Between the Library and the Laboratory: The Language of Chemistry in Eighteenth-Century France.* Baltimore: Johns Hopkins University Press, 1984.

Bachelard, Gaston. *La Formation de l'esprit scientifique.* Paris: Vrin, 1938.

Barthes, Roland. *Le Bruissement de la langue. Essais critiques IV.* Paris: Seuil, 1984.

_____. "Discours de l'histoire." *Information sur les sciences sociales,* IV (August

1967): 65-75. Rept. in *Le Bruissement de la langue*. Paris: Seuil, 1984. Pp. 53-66.
_____. "De l'œuvre au texte." *Revue d'Esthétique*. 24-25/3 (1971), 225-232.
_____. "Introduction à l'analyse structurale des récits." *Communications*, 8 (1966), 1-27. Rept. in *L'Analyse structurale du récit*. Paris: Seuil, 1981. Pp. 7-33.
_____. "Science versus Literature." In *Introduction to Structuralism*. Ed. Michael Lane. New York: Harper, 1970. 410-16. Rept. *Times Literary Supplement*, 28 September 1967. Also rept. as "De la science à la littérature" in *Le Bruissement de la langue*. Paris: Seuil, 1984. Pp. 13-20.
_____. *S/Z*. Paris: Seuil, 1970.
_____. "To Write: An Intransitive Verb?" In *The Structuralist Controversy*. Ed. R. Macksey and E. Donato. Baltimore: Johns Hopkins Press, 1970. 134-56.
Baudelaire, Charles. *Les Fleurs du mal*. Ed. Ernst Raynard. Paris: Garnier, 1958.
Belaval, Yvon. *L'Esthétique sans paradoxe de Diderot*. Paris: Gallimard, 1950.
_____. "Sur le matérialisme de Diderot." *Europaische Aufklarung. H. Dieckmann. Zum 60. Geburtstag*. Wilhelm Fink Verlag, 1967. Pp. 9-21.
Benveniste, Emile. *Problèmes de linguistique générale*. 2 vols. Paris: Gallimard, 1966.
Carr, J. L. "Pygmalion and the Philosophes: The Animated Statue in Eighteenth-Century France." *Warburg and Courtauld Inst.* (July-December 1960), 239-55.
Cassirer, Ernest. *The Philosophy of the Enlightenment*. Princeton: Princeton University Press, 1951.
Chouillet, Jacques. *La Formation des idées esthétiques de Diderot 1745-1763*. Paris: Colin, 1973.
Crocker, Lester. *Diderot's Chaotic Order: An Approach to Synthesis*. Princeton: Princeton University Press, 1974.
De Man, Paul. "Nietzsche's Theory of Rhetoric." *Symposium*, 28-29 (1974-75), 33-51.
_____. "La Structure intentionnelle de l'image romantique." *Revue Internationale de la Philosophie*. 14 (1960), 68-84.
_____. "Theory of Metaphor in Rousseau's Second Discourse." *Studies in Romanticism*. 12 (Spring 1976), 475-98.
Derrida, Jacques. *De la grammatologie*. Paris: Editions de Minuit, 1967.
_____. *Marges de la philosophie*. Paris: Minuit, 1972.
_____. *L'Archéologie du frivole*. Paris: Galilée, 1973.
Diderot Studies. Special number on "The *Rêve de D'Alembert*: Studies by Herbert Dieckmann, Georges May and Aram Vartanian." Ed. F. A. Spear. XVII (1973).
Dieckmann, Herbert. *Cinq leçons sur Diderot*. Geneva: Droz, 1959.
_____. "Diderot's Conception of Genius." *Journal of the History of Ideas*. II, 2 (1941), 151-81.
_____. "The First Edition of Diderot's *Pensées sur l'Interprétation de la Nature*." *Isis*, LXVI (1955), 251-67.
_____. "The Influence of Francis Bacon on Diderot's *Interprétation de la Nature*." *Romanic Review*, XXXIV (1943), 303-30.
Ehrard, Jean. *L'Idée de Nature en France dans la première moitié du XVIIIe siècle*. Paris: Imprimeries Réunies, 1963. Vol. II.
Fontenay, Elizabeth de. "Diderot Gynéconome." *Digraphe*, 7 (1976), 29-50.

Foucault, Michel. *L'Archéologie du savoir*. Paris: Seuil, 1969.

———. *Les Mots et les choses: une archéologie des sciences humaines*. Paris: Gallimard, 1966.

France, Peter. *Rhetoric and Truth in France: Descartes to Diderot*. Oxford: Oxford University Press, 1942.

Fried, Michael. *Absorption and Theatricality, Painting and Beholder in the Age of Diderot*. Berkeley: University of California Press, 1980.

———. "Absorption: A Master Theme in Eighteenth-Century French Painting." *Eighteenth-Century Studies*. IX, 2 (Winter 1975-76), 139-77.

———. "Toward a Supreme Fiction: Genre and Beholder in the Art Criticism of Diderot and his Contemporaries." *New Literary History*, VI, 3 (Spring 1975), 544-84.

Gay, Peter, ed. *Eighteenth-Century Studies*. Hanover, N.H.: University Press of New England, 1972.

Genette, Gérard. "Les frontières du récit." In *Figures II*. Paris: Seuil, 1969. Rept. in *L'Analyse structurale du récit*. Paris: Seuil, 1981. Pp. 158-69.

———. *Mimologiques*. Paris: Seuil, 1976.

Givner, David. "Scientific Preconceptions in Locke's Philosophy of Language." *The Journal of the History of Ideas*. 23 (July-September 1962), 340-54.

Goux, Jean-Joseph. "Descartes et la perspective." *L'Esprit Créateur*, XXV, 1 (Spring 1985), 10-21.

Gusdorf, Georges. *L'Avènement des sciences humaines au siècle des lumières*. Paris: Payot, 1973.

Greimas, Alexandre J. "Des accidents dans les sciences dites humaines: Analyse d'un texte de Georges Dumezil." *Versus*. Milan: Bompiani, 1976.

Hamon, Philippe. "Métalangage et littérature." *Poétique* 31 (1977), 261-84.

Hunt, H. J. "Logic and Linguistics." *MLR* XXXIII (1938), 215-33.

Jakobson, Roman. *Essais linguistiques*. Trans. française. 2 vols. Paris: Minuit, 1963.

———. "Qu'est-ce que la poésie?" *Questions de poétique*. Paris: Seuil, 1973.

Josephs, Herbert. *Diderot's Dialogue of Language and Gesture: Le Neveu de Rameau*. Columbus: Ohio State University Press, 1969.

——— and Jack Undank, eds. *Diderot: Digression and Dispersion*. Lexington: French Forum, 1984.

Koyré, Alexandre. *Etudes d'histoire de la pensée scientifique*. Paris: Presses Universitaires de France, 1966. Rept. Gallimard, 1973.

Lefebvre, Henri. *Diderot*. Paris: Les Editeurs Réunis, 1949.

Luc, Jean. *Diderot*. Paris: Editions Sociales Internationales, 1938.

May, Georges. *Quatres visages de Diderot*. Paris: Boivin et Cie., 1951.

Mayer, Jean. *Diderot, homme de science*. Paris: Imprimerie Bretonne, 1959.

Mortier, Roland. "Diderot au carrefour de la poésie et de la philosophie." *Revue des Sciences Humaines*. 112 (1963), 485-501.

O'Meara, Maureen. "*Le Taureau Blanc* and the Activity of Language." *Studies on Voltaire and the Eighteenth Century*. 148 (1976), 115-75.

Pappas, John, ed. *Essays on Diderot and the Enlightenment in Honor of Otis Fellows*.

Geneva: Droz, 1974.

Poulet, Georges. *Etudes sur le temps humain*. Paris: Union Générale des Editeurs, 1950.

Proust, Jacques. "Diderot et les problèmes du langage." *Romanische Forschungen.* 79 (1967), 2-27.

Pucci, Suzanne, ed. *Diderot in the Wake of Modern Critical Thought*. Spec. no. of *L'Esprit Créateur*, XXIV, no. 1 (Spring 1984).

_____. "Metamorphosis and Metaphor in Diderot's *Rêve de D'Alembert*: Pygmalion Materialized," *Symposium*. (Winter 1981-82), 225-40.

_____. "The Art, Nature and Fiction of Diderot's Beholder." *Stanford French Review*, VIII (Fall 1984), 273-94.

Roger, Jacques. "Diderot et Buffon en 1749." *Diderot Studies*, 4 (1963), 221-36.

_____. *Les Sciences de la vie dans la pensée française du dix-huitième siècle*. Paris: Colin, 1963.

Rousset, Jean. *Narcisse romancier: Essai sur la première personne dans le roman*. Paris: Corti, 1973.

Sahlin, Guvnor. *César Chesneau Dumarsais et son rôle dans l'évolution de la Grammaire Générale*. Paris: Presses Universitaires de France, 1928.

Schwartz, Jerome. *Diderot and Montaigne: The "Essais" and the Shaping of Diderot's Humanism*. Geneva: Droz, 1966.

Spear, Frederick Alfred, ed. "The *Rêve de D'Alembert*: Studies by Herbert Dieckmann, Georges May and Aram Vartanian." *Diderot Studies*, XVII (1973).

_____. *Bibliographie de Diderot. Répertoire analytique international*. Geneva: Droz, 1980.

Spitzer, Leo. *Linguistics and Literary History*. Princeton: Princeton University Press, 1948.

Starobinski, Jean. "Diderot et la parole des Autres." *Critique*. 296 (1972), 3-22.

_____. "Le Philosophe, le Géometre, l'hybride." *Poétique*. 21 (1973), 8-23.

_____. *Le Relation critique*. Paris: Gallimard, 1970.

Steadman, John M. "Beyond Hercules: Bacon and the Scientist as Hero." *Studies in the Literary Imagination*. 4 (1971-74), 3-47.

Undank, Jack, and Herbert Josephs, eds. *Diderot: Digression and Dispersion*. Lexington: French Forum, 1984.

Vartanian, Aram. *Diderot and Descartes*. Princeton: Princeton University Press, 1953.

Venturi, Franco. *La Jeunesse de Diderot: de 1713 à 1753*. Trans. J. Bertrand. Paris: Skira, 1939.

Wilson, Arthur. *Diderot: The Testing Years, 1713-1759*. New York: Oxford University Press, 1957.

Index